Why Study the Middle Ages?

PAST IMPERFECT

See further
www.arc-humanities.org/our-series/pi

Why Study the Middle Ages?

Kisha G. Tracy

ARCHUMANITIES PRESS

British Library Cataloguing in Publication Data
A catalogue record for this book is available from the British Library

© 2022, Arc Humanities Press, Leeds

ISBN (print) 9781641891974
e-ISBN (PDF) 9781802700701
e-ISBN (EPUB) 9781802700718

www.arc-humanities.org
Printed and bound in the UK (by CPI Group [UK] Ltd), USA (by Bookmasters), and elsewhere using print-on-demand technology.

Contents

Introduction

The Middle Ages and the Liberal Arts[*]

[I]f you look at them in the light of the other things to which they are joined, and if you begin to weigh them in their whole context, you will see that they are as necessary as they are fitting. Some things are to be known for their own sakes, but others, although for their own sakes they do not seem worthy of our labor, nevertheless, because without them the former class of things cannot be known with complete clarity, must by no means be carelessly skipped. Learn everything; you will see afterwards that nothing is superfluous.

Hugh of Saint Victor, Didascalicon[1]

---

[*] Parts of this book have drawn on earlier presentations, in particular at the "Healers and Killers" series at the Tower Hill Botanical Garden in Boylson, Massachusetts, on February 23, 2019; at the University of Central Oklahoma Medieval Society on November 12, 2020; and an article prepared for the Fitchburg State University LGBTQ campus newsletter, Spring 2021. I thank the participants and audience of these and other similar discussions, as too the anonymous peer-reviewer and acquisitions editors from Arc Humanities Press.

[1] Hugh of Saint Victor, *The Didascalicon*, trans. Taylor, 137. Short-form citations such as this are given where the work is cited in full in the Further Reading at the end or, if not there, in an earlier footnote. To ease reading, where a work is recurrently cited the pagination is provided parenthetically within the main body of the text.

Students and teachers of the premodern are often asked to answer the question about the relevance of these subjects, particularly by skeptics who might doubt such relevance exists. Relevance, however, has certain associations. In particular, it infers a focus on the modern, indeed sometimes to the point of excluding anything that seemingly doesn't have a readily-obvious "purpose" in modern life or to a presentist point of view. Due to that bias, the more productive conversation is one of significance. Instead of considering whether the study of the premodern is appropriate, rather we should think about its worthiness for study. Instead of defending, we should provide evidence. As Hugh of Saint Victor wrote in the eleventh century, "Nothing is superfluous." We just need to find its meaning.

Liberal Arts in the Middle Ages

In preparing to teach a course focused on the definition and value of the liberal arts and sciences, I began reading Fareed Zakaria's *In Defense of a Liberal Education*. From the beginning, I admired its accessibility for a general audience, but then reaching its second chapter on the history of liberal education, I came across this phrase that followed a paragraph on Alcuin and the court of Charlemagne: "Even during the Dark Ages, medieval monasteries kept alive a tradition of learning and inquiry."[2] My immediate response was one of indignation. First, there was the use of that phrase medievalists despise: the Dark Ages.[3] To add insult to injury, there was that damning addition of "even," as if the very idea of learning in the Middle Ages is impossible to imagine. The chapter continues with a paragraph on the influence of Islam, which is a welcome addition as the contributions of medieval Islamic civilization are not always acknowledged. But then Zakaria returns to the previous theme: "By the late Middle Ages,

---

2 Zakaria, *In Defense of a Liberal Education*, 44–45.

3 For a debunking of the use of "Dark Ages," see Gabriele and Perry, *The Bright Ages*.

Europe's stagnation was ending" (45). The following brief discussion over-emphasizes what Zakaria calls the "religious influence" (46) of the time that, in his view, *limited* education. This observation is followed by a quick turn to "Renaissance humanism." This assessment—or rather dismissal—of the medieval raises questions about how the Middle Ages is represented in histories of the liberal arts.

The answer to those questions is disheartening. There is no shortage of writings on the definition, the development, and the defense of the liberal arts, as a whole and in its parts; however, in these works, especially those meant for general audiences—as in Zakaria's otherwise excellent book—the Middle Ages is often overlooked, given limited (or limiting) discussion, or summarily dismissed, usually for its supposedly religious exclusivity. Martha Nussbaum's *Cultivating Humanity*, for instance, relegates medieval education and liberal arts to something that Renaissance humanists "react[ed] against" in order to "promot[e] a more human-centered view of the world."[4] In Mark William Roche's brief introduction in *Why Choose the Liberal Arts?*, he moves straight from Sophocles and the classical thinkers to the Enlightenment. Even when a focus on the Middle Ages is present in books not specifically written by medievalists, it tends to be hyper-focused—and frequently misattributed to the classical rather than the twelfth and thirteenth centuries—on the trivium (grammar, logic, and rhetoric), the quadrivium (arithmetic, geometry, music, and astronomy), or the seven arts as a whole, such as in Ravi Jain and Kevin Clark's *The Liberal Arts Tradition*. The history of these subject groupings, while important, are only a portion of the story and sometimes serve more to highlight differences between the medieval and contemporary periods than the continuities.

In his twelfth-century defense of the trivium, *The Metalogicon*, John of Salisbury avers: "The liberal arts are said

---

4 Martha C. Nussbaum, *Cultivating Humanity: A Classical Defense of Reform in Liberal Education* (Cambridge, MA: Harvard University Press, 1997), 103.

to have become so efficacious among our ancestors, who studied them diligently, that they enabled them to comprehend everything they read, elevated their understanding to all things, and empowered them to cut through the knots of all problems possible of solution."[5] We can note here that all seven of the disciplines in the trivium and quadrivium are called "arts," speaking to a different understanding of the rather limited use of the word today; the same is true of "sciences." The understanding of all these categories of knowledge have shifted over time, although preserved in the main concept of the liberal arts. In the *Didascalicon*, Hugh of Saint Victor distinguishes science as a "matter of use" and art as a "matter of rules and precepts":

> All sciences, indeed, were matters of use before they became matters of art. But when men subsequently considered that use can be transformed into art, and what was previously vague and subject to caprice can be brought into order by definite rules and precepts, they began, we are told, to reduce to art the habits which had arisen partly by chance, partly by nature [...] Before there was grammar, men both wrote and spoke; before there wad dialectic, they distinguished the true from the false by reasoning; before there was rhetoric, they discoursed upon civil laws; before there was arithmetic, there was knowledge of counting; before there was an art of music, they sang; before there was geometry, they measured fields; before there was astronomy, they marked off periods of time from the courses of the stars. But then came the arts, which, though they took their rise in usage, nonetheless excel it (trans. Taylor, 59–60).

He makes the further distinction that knowledge is "art when it treats of matters that only resemble the true and are objects of opinion; and discipline when, by means of true arguments, it deals with matters unable to be other than they are" (61–62). In the modern American context, the quadrivium—arithmetic, geometry, music, and astronomy—would,

5 John of Salisbury, *The Metalogicon*, trans. McGarry, 36.

with the exception of music, fall into the category of STEM—science, technology, engineering, and mathematics. To Hugh and other medieval thinkers, music as well as the rest of the disciplines in the quadrivium are part of mathematics.

Islamic thinkers, such as the tenth-century al-Farabi, known as the "Second Teacher" behind Aristotle, had similar approaches to classifications of knowledge, with some key differences. For one, instead of classifying them all under "arts," al-Farabi identifies them all as "sciences." His categories are: language (syntax, grammar, pronunciation, and poetry), logic, introductory sciences (arithmetic, geometry, astrology, music, weights, tool-making), physics (nature) and metaphysics (god), and society (jurisprudence and rhetoric).[6] The fourteenth-century scholar Ibn Khaldûn, known for creating foundations in history, sociology, ethnography, and economics, divided knowledge into logic, natural knowledge (medicine and agriculture), metaphysics (magic and the occult), quantity (geometry, arithmetic, music, and astronomy), the Qur'an and the Hadith, jurisprudence, theology, Sufism, and linguistics (grammar, lexicography, and literature).[7] Music is included with other mathematics as in the quadrivium, and it is also worth noting the inclusion of rhetoric, the art of argument and persuasion such as those often taught in college composition courses, as a science of society by al-Farabi.

Scholars will at times use distinctions to emphasize the differences between the medieval understanding of knowledge from the modern or between different cultures. While true, such an approach does a disservice to the connections that still remain. For instance, there is a parallel to be made between the quadrivium and the movement in K-12 (kindergarten to grade 12 education) to change STEM to STEAM—science, technology, engineering, arts, and mathematics.

---

6 Nasr, *Science and Civilization in Islam*, 61–62.

7 Nasr, *Science and Civilization in Islam*, 63–64. See Ibn Khaldun, *The Muqaddimah*, trans. Franz Rosenthal, accessed April 15, 2022, http://www.muslimphilosophy.com/ik/Muqaddimah/.

Non-Western views are far more acknowledging of the medieval in the history of the liberal arts. In addition to the Arabic influence mentioned previously, which is echoed by the representation of premodern Islamic education by Malika Zeghal in "The Multiple Faces of Islamic Education in a Secular Age," African influence was also essential, particularly that of the Amazigh, Augustine of Hippo. Grant Lilford focuses heavily on precolonial African universities and traditional knowledge that "blur[red] the disciplinary boundaries that have been a feature of European education since Aristotle."[8] Lilford argues that the specialty-focused modern African education system would be better served—"at its best, it engages with the precolonial past, across the national boundaries that are the most pernicious colonial legacy" (208)— returning to its medieval roots, one that "supplies writing, analytical, lifelong learning and creative skills that apply to a number of work environments," (189) which stems from the precolonial focus on "general technical and cultural knowledge while providing for specialist skills in such areas as metallurgy, medicine, poetry, music, and the arts and crafts" (191). Despite that the "liberal arts" today is regarded as an American education phenomenon,[9] Lilford rightly notes that "the conversation [about the liberal arts] has flowed around and across continents" (194). There is a significant medieval moment to this flow among continents that contributed to the shape of contemporary liberal arts.

The development of the liberal arts in the Middle Ages is intertwined with the creation of the university. "Every soci-

---

8 Grant Lilford, "The Liberal Arts in Anglophone Africa," *The Journal of General Education* 61, no. 3 (2012): 189–210 at 190. A similar version appears in "The African Liberal Arts: Heritage, Challenges, and Prospects," in *The Evolution of Liberal Arts in the Global Age*, ed. Peter Marber and Daniel Araya (New York: Routledge, 2017), 150–63.

9 Kara A. Godwin, "Precis of a Global Liberal Education Phenomenon: The Empirical Story," in *The Evolution of Liberal Arts in the Global Age*, ed. Peter Marber and Daniel Araya (New York: Routledge, 2017): 87–105 at 88.

ety," according to John Van Engen, "has devised means to educate its young and to prepare a next generation of leaders. Not every society has had universities. These guilds of scholars and students, the invention of twelfth-century Europe, receive the highest acclaim from modern scholars."[10] This common assertion that the university was born in medieval Europe is contested by the historical evidence of universities in medieval Africa. UNESCO identifies the University of al-Qarawiyyin in Fez, Morocco, as the oldest university in the world.[11] This university was founded by Fatima bint Muhammad Al-Fihriya Al-Qurashiya in 859, demonstrating the role of women benefactors. Madrasas, educational institutions, systemized in Islamic communities in the eleventh century "taught Islamic sciences—which were intended to foster the study of Islamic religious law—through a professional body of teachers, and were equipped with a structure for lodging their students."[12] Essentially, they became colleges. In the eleventh century, Nizam al-Mulk, Vizier of the Seljuq Empire, created madrasas in Baghdad, Naishapur, and other cities.[13] Madrasas issued written documents (diplomas), called *ijaza*, that signified a student's accomplishments,[14] and the University of al-Qarawiyyin is considered by many to be the first degree-granting institution.

What about the influence of the institution of the Church, especially as it was heavily involved in and heavily invested in the European university's production of students versed in theology? There is no doubt that the Christian Church

---

10 Van Engen, "Introduction," in *Learning Institutionalized*, ed. Van Engen, 1.

11 "Medina of Fez," United Nations Educational, Scientific, and Cultural Organization, accessed April 15, 2022, http://whc.unesco.org/en/list/170.

12 Malika Zeghal, "The Multiple Faces of Islamic Education in a Secular Age," in *Islam in the Modern World*, ed. Jeffrey T. Kenney and Ebrahim Moosa (New York: Routledge, 2014), 125–47 at 128.

13 Nasr, *Science and Civilization in Islam*, 71.

14 Zeghal, "The Multiple Faces of Islamic Education," 129.

asserted its influence over European universities. We can look at this from different perspectives. We can consider this restrictive; there were certainly teachers who were accused and condemned for their teachings, which supports considering the Church's influence in this light. We can also consider other possibilities, such as the effect of this influence on the university responsibility to society. Jacques Verger states, "[T]he church imposed on universities the idea that the mere love of science, the pure research of truth, could not be the only aim of learning. Learning had to carry out two other requirements: it had to be socially useful [...] and it had to respect and even support religious orthodox as defined by the papacy."[15] Here we have these two ideas in one context. Learning had to go beyond study for the sake of society and it had to support orthodox beliefs—service to the community and restriction at one and the same time. James Weisheipl emphasizes that "Masters could lecture on any book they chose and they could hold any opinion not directly opposed to the Christian faith. Students could choose any master they wished to work under."[16] The sense of academic freedom exists in the ability of teachers to shape their own curriculum and of students to choose their own instructors, not to mention the prominent practice of university personnel maintaining autonomy and authority over their own members, but with the caveat that the opinions expressed must not oppose "Christian faith."

This is not unique to the European Middle Ages. For instance, the Islamic madrasas were "most of the time sustained by a waqf (religious endowment) deed and therefore by individual or family patronage that could also be linked

15 Jacques Verger, "The First French Universities and the Institutionalization of Learning," in *Learning Institutionalized: Teaching in the Medieval University*, ed. John Van Engen (Notre Dame: University of Notre Dame Press, 2000), 5–19 at 13.

16 James A. Weisheipl, "The Structure of the Arts Faculty in the Medieval University," *British Journal of Educational Studies* 19, no. 3 (1971): 263–71 at 271.

to the world of politics," and such patronage "allowed the founders to specify the domains of instruction."[17] Almost any institution in any culture of any time period, especially if it is reliant upon patronage (including modern colleges—think, for instance, about the convention of naming college buildings after donors), has political ties of one type or another that affect its workings. That the Western (Roman) Church did so is not a reason to disqualify the significance of the period's contributions to education. As a counter to the belief that everything was controlled, note that, the *Authentica habita*, written ca. 1155 by Emperor Frederick I Barbarossa and considered the founding document of the first European university in Bologna, granted scholars freedom of movement as well as freedom from monetary reprisal.[18] This document is considered the foundation and a long-standing argument for the modern concept of academic freedom, which theoretically allows instructors in higher education to use their expertise to select topics of study for students without pressure from outside influences, and served as a principal source for the Magna Charta of the European Universities signed in 1986 that declared universal academic freedom.[19]

Indeed, freedom is essential to the idea of the "liberal arts." Zakaria writes:

> Basic skills for sustenance were no longer sufficient—citizens also had to be properly trained to run their own society. The link between a broad education and liberty became important to the Greeks. Describing this approach to instruction centuries later, the Romans coined a term for

---

17 Zeghal, "The Multiple Faces of Islamic Education," 128.

18 Paolo Nardi, "Chapter 3: Relations with Authority," in *A History of the University in Europe: Volume 1, Universities in the Middle Ages*, ed. H. de Ridder-Symoens (Cambridge: Cambridge University Press, 1992), 77–107.

19 "Read the Magna Charta Universitatum," Observatory Magna Charta Universitatum, accessed April 15, 2022, http://www.magna-charta.org/magna-charta-universitatum/read-the-magna-charta/the-magna-charta.

it: a "liberal" education, using the word *liberal* in its original Latin sense, "of or pertaining to free men" (41–42).

The image of a "free person" having the ability and means to participate in education echoes through time. Ibn Khaldun claims that knowledge only flourishes in "sedentary culture" and the "luxury they enjoy" because it is "something additional to just making a living."[20] In reference to his education reform plan, Alfred the Great wrote in his Old English ninth-century preface to the translation of Gregory the Great's *Pastoral Care*: "with God's help we may very easily do if we have peace, so that all the youth of free men now in England who have the means to apply themselves to it, be set to learning, while they are not useful for any other occupation."[21] The definition of *freedom*, however, evolved. John of Salisbury stated that the liberal arts "are called 'liberal,' either because the ancients took care to have their children instructed in them; or because their object is to effect man's liberation, so that, freed from cares, he may devote himself to wisdom."[22] This application of "liberal" is far more individual and less about the surrounding society, although certainly John of Salisbury recognized the connection of the liberal arts to bigger concerns.

Middle Ages in the Liberal Arts

As much as I might like to at times, I cannot require that everyone love the Middle Ages—indeed, that passion cannot be commanded nor would I seriously want it to be—but I would encourage spending time thinking about why a thorough understanding of the past is so critical to the liberal

---

20 Ibn Khaldun, *The Muqaddimah*, chap. 6, §8.

21 Alfred, "Translation of Alfred's Prose Preface to Pastoral Care," Bucknell University, accessed April 15, 2022, http://www.departments.bucknell.edu/english/courses/engl440/pastoral/translation.shtml.

22 John of Salisbury, *The Metalogicon*, trans. McGarry, 37.

arts. For instance, we should consider the ideas that civilization has been advanced not by a single ethnicity, but through diversity; that concepts such as gender and disability are social constructs and have been/are malleable; that humanity excels in its complexity, not simplicity. These are exercises I recommend for anyone engaging in a liberal education.

The modern liberal arts are separated into three categories, or cultures, as expanded from the two delineated by C. P. Snow in 1959: humanities, STEM, and (the newer one) social sciences.[23] These three categories provide the structure of this book. Taking these categories as a whole, Kara Godwin consolidates definitions of the liberal arts, identifying three essential parts: multidisciplinarity, a "general education" component, and a focus on "elemental skills that include critical thinking, problem-solving, analysis, communication, global citizenship, quantitative and qualitative literacy, and/or a sense of social responsibility."[24] Patrick Awuah, co-founder of Ashesi University in Ghana, defines liberal arts as more active, as "asking the right questions and looking at issues from multiple perspectives and thinking critically and thinking analytically, both qualitatively and quantitatively."[25] According to the Association of American Colleges and Universities (AAC&U), a "Liberal Education is an approach to learning that empowers individuals and prepares them to deal with complexity, diversity, and change" and should be emphasized "across the entire educational continuum—from school through college—at progressively higher levels of achievement."[26] Examining aspects of these definitions

---

23 See Kagen, *The Three Cultures*.

24 Godwin, "Precis of a Global Liberal Education," 88.

25 Elizabeth Redden, "A Liberal Arts College Marks Five Years in Ghana," *Inside Higher Ed*, October 19, 2007, https://www.insidehighered.com/news/2007/10/19/liberal-arts-college-marks-five-years-ghana.

26 "What Is Liberal Education?," *Association of American Colleges & Universities*, accessed June 23, 2022, https://www.aacu.org/leap/what-is-a-liberal-education.

reveals the place of the Middle Ages in the liberal arts that are at the heart of most general education programs.

Quite often, when talking to a medievalist, you will hear them say that the study of the Middle Ages is fundamentally interdisciplinary. Far from a boast (although at times it might be), it is a truth of the field. Medieval literature scholars differ from their counterparts in other time periods in that we consider almost all written text, despite genre, as our purview, which means we must bring to bear various disciplines in the course of our study. Art historians must be able to draw on religion, literature, science, among other fields. Disability studies research encompasses science, medicine, literature, sociology, linguistics, and archaeology. To complete our work, medievalists must be at the least multidisciplinary, working with various fields, and more likely interdisciplinary, connecting those fields together.

Westmont College, in Santa Barbara, California began using brain scans to test the efficacy of study abroad programs, attempting to prove that students who study abroad demonstrate higher levels of aptitude and, more importantly, an increase in abilities to work with diverse peoples.[27] While the methodology of this study is controversial, its hypothesis is well-taken. I would argue that it is just as vital to immerse ourselves in the otherness of past cultures as well as modern ones. To increase contact with the artists of other times, to struggle with putting ourselves in their minds and daily lives, to think in their languages, to imagine the scope of and reasons for their wars gives us the opportunity to immerse ourselves in other mindsets and beliefs. It is only through contact with others that we discover who we are, tease out what is human, and develop tolerance, empathy, and acceptance. In addition, there is perhaps no better time period than the Middle Ages to juxtapose with our own in order to consider

---

27 Colleen Murphy, "One College's Method to Prove Its Value: Scanning Students' Brains," *Chronicle of Higher Education,* June 4, 2015, http://www.chronicle.com/article/One-College-s-Method-to/230661.

these issues. There are a multitude of examples in the contact among cultures and in how its varying forms negotiate and are negotiated by society.[28]

Milton McC. Gatch in "The Medievalist and Cultural Literacy" writes:

> Perhaps at the core of many of the social, economic, educational, and intellectual problems that face us today is our deep, nearly unconscious commitment to the notion that history is progress, that the human community moves inexorably and endlessly towards betterment, sophistication, wisdom, happiness, and that the future will be preferable to the past [...]. Those of us involved in historical studies need to be introducing cautions about the doctrines of progress. It should be stressed that past cultures were sophisticated in ways that often outstrip us.[29]

This passage captures my experience as a student of literature and history, an instructor, a citizen, and even a social media onlooker. There is a distinct tendency to believe that what is past—especially what is long past and thus different than our present view—must be "primitive" or even "wrong." There is a general belief that the peoples of the past were somehow exempt from (positive, especially) human nature, had less of a sense of morality (by any definition) than we do now, or were unaware of basic human dilemmas or triumphs. This approach to history often creates—wittingly or unwittingly—a "better than thou" attitude and a stagnant complacency. The Middle Ages in particular seems to draw these sorts of conclusions: dogmatic slaves to faith, universal abusers of women, staunch deniers of science, As Sonja Drimmer laments, "[I]t's the presentism that such an attitude cultivates. If c500–1500 Europe was the 'Dark Ages,' then that which succeeded was 'enlightened.' Think of the enormous danger in subscribing to that belief."[30] Relegating this

---

28 See Klimek et al., *Global Medieval Contexts*.

29 McC. Gatch, "The Medievalist and Cultural Literacy," 595.

30 Sonja Drimmer, "To add to this...," Twitter, May 27, 2019, https://

time period to "primitive" distances us from close examination of what has not changed in society or, if it has changed, that it might not indeed be for the better. "If we can learn to critically think about medieval culture," Brandon Hawk theorizes, "we can learn to critically think about any culture."[31] For instance, if what we have been taught about this culture is wrong, what else is also incorrect? If we can learn to appreciate the nuances of this culture, then what can we discover about our own? If we can develop an empathy for the peoples far removed from us, what empathy can we feel for modern peoples? Certainly, the study of the Middle Ages—especially in a broad integration in the liberal arts, "across the entire educational continuum" as per the AAC&U—is a way to improve modern society.

In order to demonstrate the integration of the Middle Ages across the disciplines and, more importantly, articulate the significance of studying the period, especially in the limitations of a volume of this size, I will highlight two interdisciplinary threads in each of the succeeding chapters: disability studies, such as disability representation in literary texts, accommodations, and museum representations, and diversity studies, such as (mis)appropriations of the Middle Ages by white supremacists, scientific and DNA studies, and what a global Middle Ages looks like.

While medieval disability studies is a relatively new field, coming into its own in the late 2000s with the creation of the scholarly organization Society for the Study of Disability in the Middle Ages, disability studies as a whole has a longer history with the first academic journal, *The Disability Studies Quarterly*, established in the 1980s. The passage of the Americans with Disabilities Act (ADA) in 1990 initiated the creation

---

twitter.com/Sonja_Drimmer/status/1133032541429145600? fbclid=IwAR36NY2nrT3W_ucs76zBnyeNKjAEi1oFyCmrwyDujoEi MO21-kE9v3XG3zE.

31 Brandon Hawk, "In general, I firmly believe…," Facebook, January 18, 2016, https://www.facebook.com/groups/939478049471496/permalink/956751301077504/.

of a number of academic programs across the United States. My own university, Fitchburg State in Massachusetts, created a disability studies minor in the 2010s, offering a "liberal arts approach [...] of the historical, social, aesthetic, literary, legal, educational, philosophical, biological and political framing of disability."[32] Other disability studies minors, like that at University of California Berkeley, place more of an emphasis on the history of disability, examining its construction as a "historical constant," which speaks to the significance of studying medieval disability.[33]

In disability studies, scholars often debate the merits of studying disability through the lens of various models, especially the medical and social, that can be used to understand and engage with disability and impairment. I prefer, however, to think of these as approaches to disability rather than models unto themselves, more following the inclusive cultural model outlined by Sharon Snyder and David Mitchell. As they state, "[t]he definition of disability must incorporate both the outer and inner reaches of culture and experience as a combination of profoundly social and biological forces."[34] While each of the approaches to disability are not confined to specific disciplines, and are themselves intertwined with each other as individually they do not present a complete image of disability, for the purpose of this discussion, I will focus specifically on one in each chapter—religious (important to medieval studies), medical, and social—in order to explicate what those concepts look like within those disciplines and how they bridge a study of the medieval period with the modern era.

Diversity studies is, in comparison, a far more amorphous category. With a vast array of definitions, it is difficult to

---

32 "Disability Studies Minor," Fitchburg State University, accessed April 15, 2022, https://www.fitchburgstate.edu/academics/undergraduate/undergraduate-day-programs/all-minors/disability-studies-minor-new-fall-2012/.

33 "Disability Studies," University of California Berkeley, accessed April 15, 2022, https://disability-studies.ugis.berkeley.edu/.

34 Snyder and Mitchell, *Cultural Locations of Disability*, 7.

pin down; however, typically, diversity studies involves the examination of cultural and human interactions with the goal of decreasing inequalities and disparities across the span of differences. It often includes ethnicity, gender, age, disability, economic, among other, studies internal and external to the home culture. There are a number of related terms—global competence, world perspective, civics, inclusivity, global citizenry, etc.—that are often included in diversity studies, some of which are more problematic than others. Using global competence as his starting point, Ohio State Education professor Emmanuel Jean Francois provides a useful discussion of the bigger picture:

> I believe that the world is a global village of unique diverse communities, and that the diversity of these multiple communities makes it a challenge for individuals to navigate from their community through another community that may, in many cases, be significantly different. Therefore, as citizens of this global village, we should acquire a certain level of global competence in order to function productively and responsibly. I define global competence based on the awareness, knowledge, skills, and attitudes that an individual should continuously develop regarding the world, including its various societies, people, cultures, issues, challenges, and opportunities.[35]

We will see that awareness, knowledge, skills, and attitudes are all integral to medieval diversity studies.

In only a cursory examination of diversity studies majors and minors offered in universities and colleges across the United States, it is significant that they are often described as preparation for a wide spectrum of careers that involve work with a variety of populations, notably running the gamut of the humanities, STEM, and the social sciences. For instance, Missouri State lists their minor in diversity studies as preparation for "business, industry, education, social welfare,

---

35 Cited in Dawn Bikowski and Talinn Phillips, *Teaching with a Global Perspective: Practical Strategies from Course Design to Assessment* (New York: Routledge, 2019), 182.

health and medicine."[36] Similarly, for their diversity studies minor, the University of Texas Arlington identifies careers in "business, industry, education, social welfare, mental health, and health."[37] For their certificate in diversity studies, Penn State lists "human resources, non-profit agencies, social welfare, education, and health and medicine."[38]

It is easy enough to make these claims, but the real question is *how* diversity studies prepares learners for these careers. To make this connection, it's useful to turn to the stated learning outcomes of these programs. Susquehanna University in Pennsylvania articulates the goals for their minor as:

- Knowledge of the limits and contexts of one's own experience and the ability to value the different experiences of others.

- Recognition and understanding of the diversities of human experience.

- Continued growth development as a contributing member of a number of communities within human society.

- Commitment to an ongoing development of the life of the mind.[39]

---

36 "Diversity Studies," Missouri State, accessed April 15, 2022, https://www.missouristate.edu/areastudies/diversitystudies/default.htm.

37 "Diversity Studies Minor and Certificate," University of Texas Arlington, accessed April 15, 2022, https://www.uta.edu/ssw/academics/diversity-studies/diversity-minor.php.

38 "Diversity Studies Undergraduate Certificate Program," Pennsylvania State University, accessed April 15, 2022, https://wgss.la.psu.edu/undergraduates/degree-requirements/diversity-studies-undergraduate-certificate-program.

39 "Diversity Studies," Susquehanna University, accessed April 22, 2022, https://www.susqu.edu/academics/majors-and-minors/diversity-studies/.

Penn State lists their certificate's outcomes as:

- Apply basic theories of identity, difference, social power and privilege to a wide range of textual and visual materials, and to their own interactions in the context of day-to-day life.

- Critically engage how race, gender, sexuality, class, ethnicity, and disability have been constructed in the United States.

- Consider transnational dimensions of similar dynamics and contrast these with the United States context.

- Identify and analyze the multiple ways individuals, communities, and social movements have resisted and remade categories of identity and changed relations of power over time and space.

- Recognize and explore the constructions of social identity.

As these outcomes indicate, by engaging in diversity studies, we practice critical thinking, digging beyond stated biases to determine the roots of human interaction, innovation, and, yes, even bigotry. We recognize certain broad categorizations as social constructs and perhaps faulty in their premises. We identify which long-standing beliefs have no basis in truth or reality. And we foster a culture of empathy. More often than not, variations of these outcomes appear in university courses with medieval content.

Looking at the Middle Ages through the lens of diversity studies and vice versa provides the connective tissue to understand how the issues of diversity developed and how they have been distorted in modern imaginations. One way medieval studies has sought to broaden its scope is the recent surge of interest in the global Middle Ages. In the past, the focus of medievalists has been on Europe in the rough period of 500–1500. As a result, popular understanding of the Middle Ages is that it only refers to the West, thus propagating such misapprehensions like the attribution of the first university. The field is now asking more widely: what about the rest of the cultures and peoples around the world? Peter Frankopan, in introducing the *Journal of Medieval Worlds*, defends its creation:

> Doing so can help reclaim the "Middle Ages" in terms that allow and even force us to think about experiences, similar or otherwise, in other regions and continents and removes the Eurocentric straight-jacket of what scholars mean when they write about the medieval period [...]. Separating one country or region from others is arbitrary and myopic, as all realize; but clearly a great deal of work has to go in to exploring in more detail the rivalries, connections, and exchanges of all kinds that have encouraged an increasing number of scholars to talk about the "Global Middle Ages."[40]

In 2021, the University of California at Los Angeles (UCLA) Center for Medieval and Renaissance Studies renamed itself the CMRS Center for Early Global Studies (CMRS–CEGS). In the announcement of this change, the Dean of the Division of Humanities commented that the renamed centre "promotes the study of a multi-centered world in which methodology and comparison connect distinct areas of the globe, allowing scholars to exchange effectively from within their fields or work together innovatively across them."[41] As this idea of the global Middle Ages gains traction in the field, through changes such as this one at UCLA, we should engage in discussions of diversity studies more broadly and general education learning, bringing an understanding of the medieval to the table across fields of study. Additionally, it elevates and equalizes cultures that have traditionally been marginalized or, consciously or unconsciously, forgotten. For example, as Grant Lilford notes, "The liberal arts [...] provide a means for Africans, secure in the firm understanding of African history and society, to engage with the West not as aid recipients or

---

40 Frankopan, "Why We Need to Think About the Global Middle Ages," 9.

41 David Schaberg, "CMRS Is Now CMRS-CEGS," *UCLA*, October 13, 2021, https://cmrs.ucla.edu/news/cmrs-is-now-cmrs-cegs/.

cheap labor but as equals in the transmission and creation of wisdom."[42] Integration of medieval studies into the liberal arts—all the liberal arts—deepens our concepts of cultural interactions and pushes back against deliberate propaganda.

Jes Battis summarizes the stakes well:

> The Middle Ages were not white. They were not cis. They were not European. They were incredibly diverse and challenging and full of debate around issues of race, gender, sexuality, ability, power. They must be taught globally, inclusively, and unwoven from hatred [and] genocide.[43]

Or put more succinctly by Lisa Fagin Davis, the Executive Director of the Medieval Academy of America: the Middle Ages "were full of humans being human."[44]

---

42 Lilford, "The Liberal Arts in Anglophone Africa," 208–9.

43 Jes Battis, "The Middle Ages were not white," Twitter, June 3, 2019, https://twitter.com/jesbattis/status/113575064479759974 5?fbclid=IwAR0X53wtwHE6ToYtV885z5g8EHcyzTGRdgOZ6Wm-GxZj_C9_LNMwFpMdL-A.

44 Lisa Fagin Davis, "Please don't refer to the early Middle Ages…," Twitter, May 26, 2019, https://twitter.com/lisafdavis/status/11 32773773738946562?fbclid=IwAR1-AeDJqGQ1VYEOKrDhKE-qToKBFzWqzJ0yTvwwQPoNr75Tx1HTLdL__s4.

Chapter 1

The Middle Ages and the Humanities

I convinced myself that I hated medieval history for a long time, but it was literally just because I only learned about it in middle school and that education was all misconceptions.[1]

Without studying human beings over the course of time, we risk failing to discover what it means to be human. Our modern experience is only one of many throughout the course of our existence. Studying what we know about our counterparts in the past, how they reacted to and understood their world, and what commonalities they share with us presents a method to understand what "humanness" is. David Lunt argues that the "application of reason to understanding the events of the past allows writers and readers of history to construct, to engage with, to accept, and to refute arguments."[2] If necessary, we can add "in the present" to the end of that statement. The Middle Ages marks the final premodern period, at least in Western civilization, and the precolonial period, and, thus, is ideally situated as a site for deep

1 Kim Webb, "I convinced myself that I hated medieval history," Twitter, May 27, 2019, https://twitter.com/historygeek215/status/1133014857249447936?fbclid=IwAR2NEoojOSu_zXTDbPxH_ytcNViN0uuZBNLfTxrx5odaTTl0dA-T-OTVu-s.

2 David Lunt, "Ancient History's Contribution to Liberal Education," in Why the Humanities Matter Today, ed. Lee Trepanier and Kirk Fitzpatrick (Lanham: Lexington, 2017), 111–26 at 112.

investigation into past humanness. It reaches simultaneously backward to previous civilizations and forward to future generations, uniting eras and highlighting (dis)continuities.

Humanities study is, according to Helen Small, "the meaning-making practices of human culture, past and present, focusing on interpretation and critical evaluation, primarily in terms of the individual response and with an ineliminable element of subjectivity."[3] The humanities in the United States today generally refers to the collective study of literature, history, philosophy, religion, writing, languages and linguistics, and the arts. Some of these disciplines map easily to the medieval trivium—grammar, logic, and rhetoric: languages and linguistics, philosophy, and writing—and to the quadrivium—music. Although a misnomer, the phrase "humanities" is often used as a substitute for the "liberal arts" more generally. Much—too much—of the recent energy in the humanities is focused on defenses in the face of a barrage of critiques concerning the value of their study.[4] Why are the humanities important? We spend a lot of time trying to answer this question. This skepticism of the humanities in the United States is, according to Jerome Kagen, due to the American need for "intellectual work with pragmatic consequences."[5] Everything should have a practical application. The criticism is not new, however. The *Metalogicon* is a response to critics of the trivium—critiques that sound hauntingly similar to this contemporary skepticism. John of Salisbury argues: "[This critic] undermines and uproots all liberal studies, assails the whole structure of philosophy, tears to shreds humanity's social contract, and destroys the means of brotherly charity and reciprocal interchange of services."[6] My own brief argument for the humanities in general is less grandiose, but hopefully nonetheless compelling: one, it would be a dull life if every-

---

3 Small, *The Value of the Humanities*, 23.

4 Lee Trepanier succinctly describes the criticisms as well as the defenses in the introduction to *Why the Humanities Matter Today*.

5 Kagen, *The Three Cultures*, 222.

6 John of Salisbury, *The Metalogicon*, trans. McGarry, 11.

thing was about the practical alone and, two, the humanities are far more pragmatic than most realize, which, hopefully, is illustrated by this book.

A significant portion of academic medievalists work in humanities fields, which is why we are turning here first. As opposed to the STEM or social sciences categories, there is no difficulty in imagining the type of medieval subjects that fits into the humanities. The history, literature, philosophy, theology, and art of the period are staple features of the field.

It may seem counter-intuitive after the previous discussion of Milton McC. Gatch's views of "progress" to discuss faith and belief, although such a reaction is unto itself something to reconsider. Faith is an aspect of studying the Middle Ages that deserves and demands recognition. While science certainly existed in this period and some rather sophisticated thought at that, particularly in Arabic cultures, it is a time period occurring prior to what we call the scientific revolution or the age of psychoanalysis. Their worldview is frequently defined in terms of faith and belief—not the unquestioning belief that is often misattributed to the period, but, rather, deep and careful thought about the very meaning of belief and how belief can be explored, shaped, defined, and applied. It strips the trappings of "knowing" away, opening up what is possible. This is a period when, no matter how we might diagnose it, the late fourteenth-century English anchoress and mystic Julian of Norwich believes firmly in the realness of her divine visions. There is a freedom from ordinary explanation that allows for imaginative exploration.

It is from this space of potential that we derive our continued love affair with all things medieval. The medieval world is the backdrop for countless modern stories: J. R. R. Tolkien's *Lord of the Rings*, George R. R. Martin's *Game of Thrones*, Patrick Rothfuss' *Kingkiller Chronicle*, Kazuo Ishiguro's *The Buried Giant*, to name only a few. We can argue it is simply about the romance of fighting on a horse and wielding a sword, and no doubt that plays a role in the fascination, but the connection goes much deeper. The medieval period, the last premodern and precolonial period, is a perfect combination of familiarity and strangeness, a combination that ceases to be quite as balanced the further back in time we go. It is akin to a dream space, where the setting seems recognizable, yet at the same time completely alien from our everyday experience. It is stripped of those ubiquitous technological and practical items that we take for granted in modern life—cars, planes, stoves, dishwashers, plumbing, grocery stores, laptops, cell phones. In their place is imaginative possibility. Gods and angels visit mortals. Dragons sleep deep in the earth. Light pours out of the mouth of a rightful king. Skeletons give speeches. And these occurrences are not confined only to fiction, but seep into the medieval everyday world in a way that we as a collective do not experience in contemporary life, at least in the United States. That authors so frequently choose the medieval as their setting is unsurprising; the possibilities are endless, and it is not weighed down by modern memory as we can only access the real medieval through such mediums as written works and artifacts.[7]

There are dangers, however, in romanticizing any time period too much. The famous image of the "knight in shining armor," for instance, was created during the Victorian period and is the byproduct of nostalgia more than anything truly historical. A similar nostalgia—and more, obsession— surrounds the idea of the "Crusader." "The representation of the [C]rusades in the most extreme rhetoric of the present moment," Nicholas Paul tells us, "is most often drawn not from a direct engagement with medieval materials, but from centuries of modern remembering, re-assigning, and reinterpreting, much of it carried out in art and literature."[8] Depend-

---

7 See Geoffrey Mock, "Why Game of Thrones & Fantasy Literature Get Medieval: Jessica Hines on the enduring power of the Middle Ages for literary imagination," *Duke Today*, May 1, 2019, https://today.duke.edu/2019/05/why-game-thrones-fantasy-literature-get-medieval?fbclid=IwAR2QWwbL-W2ucBgglfqy11RS1Kt5ihGPcsERsDg2HHGq1NO87RxrKtTBves.

8 Nicholas L. Paul, "Modern Intolerance and the Medieval Crusades," in *Whose Middle Ages?*, edited by Andrew Albin et al. (New

ing on the propagator of the imagery, the Crusades have been an opportunity for glorification or a means of spreading fear. The glorification has led to such seemingly innocuous phenomena that in reality ignore the history and deny the distress the idea causes to many people.

In Worcester, Massachusetts, the sports teams of the College of the Holy Cross were named "The Crusaders." As an extension, so was their school newspaper. In 2018, faculty and students started to push back on this name, citing especially the fact that a KKK publication is also called *The Crusader*. The student publication decided to change its name to *The Spire*, citing their desire to "provide a platform for *all* students."[9] The day after they announced the change the college Board of Directors voted whether or not to follow suit with the mascot, a (historically inaccurate itself) knight with a sword and shield. They voted to keep the mascot. The editor of the *Worcester Magazine*, Walter Bird, Jr., praised this decision, commenting that Holy Cross "Crusaders have cast their own shadow," implying the possibility of a reclamation of Crusader imagery.[10] The Board's decision was eventually reversed by the university president.

Such division also followed when The Crusaders rugby team in Christchurch, New Zealand debated changing their name after the attack on two mosques in the city in March 2019. The white supremacist shooter wrote the names of anti-Muslim people and events on his weapons, only one of which was "Acre 1189," an infamous battle of the Third Crusade that was a loss for Muslim forces.[11] Almost immediately,

York: Fordham University Press, 2019), https://fordham.bepress.com/history/15. See also Tyerman, *The World of the Crusades*.

9 James Gallagher, "The Last of *The Crusader*," *The Spire*, February 2, 2018, https://hcspire.com/2018/02/02/last-of-the-crusaders-first-of-the-spires/.

10 Walter Bird, Jr., "Editorial: They are Crusaders," Worcester Magazine, February 8, 2018, https://www.worcestermag.com/story/opinion/editorials/2018/02/08/editorial-they-are-crusaders/10928626007/.

11 Jon Gambrell, "Rifles used in New Zealand mosque shooting

the Crusaders rugby team and New Zealand's minister for sport and recreation began talking with the Muslim community of Christchurch to consider a rebranding. Although he was more open to a change, Crusaders CEO Colin Mansbridge made a similar argument as editor Bird, commenting that the Crusaders team and its contributions to the community was "more reflective of a positive Crusade."[12] The question is: is it possible to reclaim what was already a reclaimed and reinterpreted, not to mention highly charged, history? And, if so, is it sufficient to do so through the positive reputations of a college or a sports team? In addition, is it worth doing so in the face of the trauma inflicted on particular populations?

These are the types of questions that we can explore through the study of the Middle Ages in the humanities.

Disability Studies

A religious approach to disability focuses on the connection of disability to the soul, to the divine, or to practices of faith. Medieval studies, in particular, has contributed to the understanding of this approach; as Joshua Eyler noted in a seminal volume of essays in the field, "the Middle Ages are so different from other historical eras that we need to develop new models that take into account the aspects of medieval social and religious systems that cannot be completely explained by modern constructionist models."[13] Sometimes, this religious connection takes the form of equating disability with

---

bore white supremacist references," *USA Today*, March 15, 2019, https://www.usatoday.com/story/news/world/2019/03/15/new-zealand-shootings-guns-used-bore-white-supremacist-references/3172793002/.

12 "Rugby: Crusaders and New Zealand Rugby say maintaining name along with branding 'no longer tenable'," *NZ Herald*, April 3, 2019, https://www.nzherald.co.nz/sport/news/article.cfm?c_id=4&objectid=12218936. Note: a change in name did not eventually happen.

13 *Disability in the Middle Ages*, ed. Eyler, 2.

a form of sin (your own or that of others), at other times it manifests as the holiness of suffering, and in still others it is intertwined with the concept of charity, and these are only a few of the ways disability manifests in the Middle Ages.

Saints' lives, or hagiography, are a particularly rich literary corpus for discussing disability: saints healing disabilities as they mimic Christ, experiencing disabilities themselves, and even, surprisingly enough, instigating disabilities in others. This complex depiction is often at odds with modern representations of medieval disability, which tends to reduce disability to a manifestation of sin—parallel to the all-too-common trend that reduces disability to a negative, "better off dead," view, as in the case of the controversial book and film *Me Before You*.

The ability of saints to heal is a prevalent theme through their stories. Saints are intended to represent human figures who have abilities similar to Christ, of which one is healing. Scenes in saints' lives often depict a character or characters with some form of disabling feature coming to the saint or being brought to them for treatment. Generally, there are not many details about these individuals; they are usually even nameless. Their presence in the saint's story allows the saint to prove their holiness and/or to convert those watching or reinforce their faith.

The fourteenth-century Middle English *Shorter South English Legendary Life of St. Frideswide* serves as an example of healing disability, in this case mental disability. St. Frideswide is confronted with an individual who is demonstrating erratic behavior:

> A very amazing thing happened one day
> To a fisherman who lay asleep in a boat with his companions.
> He began to rave as he woke from sleep.
> Up along his fellows, made he began to leap around,
> So that one that there was among them all he killed;
> And when he was collapsed, with his teeth he gnawed on him.
> All that could came to him and restrained him,
> And not easily with much pain they tied him up.
> They were all busy leading that foul spirit

Toward that holy maid, that she for him would pray.
The maid made the sign of the cross on his forehead;
The bound body fell down, as if it were dead.
The maid told them to untie him,
And then told him in God's name to get up, healed and sound.
Whole and sound the man arose and praised God almighty
And that maid who had delivered him from that foul
creature. (ll. 96–111)[14]

Here we have a fisherman who is raving, leaping around, killing a fellow worker, and gnawing on the body. This behavior is considered unusual to the point that they tie him up in order to control it and, seemingly, to protect him and themselves. Rather than casting him aside, they exhibit concern for their companion and seek help for him. When he is brought bound before St. Frideswide, she makes the sign of the cross on him, which causes him to fall to the ground unconscious. She unbinds the physical ties, commanding him to rise healthy, which he does. In this case, the saint is returning a character suddenly exhibiting mental illness to a state of sound mind.

In terms of experiencing disability, the fifteenth-century English *Life of Mary of Oegines* is a useful example as the beguine Marie of Oignies is portrayed with a variety of mental illness indicators, in particular fluctuating mental states, issues with food, and self-violence. Indeed, Marie characterizes her relationship to God and her faith in terms of depression:

And when she prayed specially for anybody, as with a wonderful experience our Lord showed to her and answered her spirit. Truly, she perceived meanwhile by elation of her spirit or depression whether she were heard or not. (141, ll. 44–45; 142, ll. 1–2)[15]

---

14 Translation mine from the original: *Middle English Legends of Women Saints*, ed. Sherry L Reames (Kalamazoo: Medieval Institute Publications, 2003).

15 Translation is mine and Alicia Protze's taken from Carl Horstmann, "Prosalegenden: die Legenden des MS Douce 114," *Anglia* 8 (1885): 134–84.

For Marie, it is through "elation of her spirit or depression" that she is able to gauge the success of her communication with God. In outward signs of invisible disability, the saint also frequently cries uncontrollably, and yet this experience too is couched in terms of a positive relationship with God. Her fasting, even to the point of potential eating disorders, as well as the cutting of her own skin also are represented as natural manifestations of her sainthood.

William Paris' fourteenth-century Middle English *Life of Christina* (of Bolsena) presents us with another example of a saint experiencing a disability, but also one of a saint causing disability in others. When St. Christina does not comply with her tormentor Julian's wishes, he orders her tongue cut out:

> "Cut out her tongue! It does me wrong."
> And when her tongue lay at her feet,
> She spoke all well, that bright maiden,
> As if it had never been cut from her.
> They heard and saw, all men with sight.
> She took her tongue up, where it lay,
> And then she cast it at Julian's eye,
> That always never after
> On that side was he able to see. (ll. 460-68)[16]

Instances of saints, particularly female saints, being disabled through torture are common in hagiography.[17] The process of torture reveals the saint's commitment to their beliefs. In this case, it is also an opportunity for a miracle. St. Christina

---

16 Translations mine from the original in *Middle English Legends of Women Saints*, ed. Reames.

17 See *Virgin Lives and Holy Deaths*, ed. Wogan-Browne and Burgess; Samantha J. E. Riches, "Virtue and Violence: Saints, Monsters and Sexuality in Medieval Culture," in *Medieval Sexuality: A Casebook*, ed. April Harper and Caroline Proctor (New York: Routledge, 2008), 59–78; and Anke Bernau, "A Christian Corpus: Virginity, Violence, and Knowledge in the Life of St. Katherine of Alexandria," in *St. Katherine of Alexandria: Texts and Contexts in Western Medieval Europe*, ed. Jacqueline Jenkins and Katherine J. Lewis (Turnhout: Brepols, 2003), 109–30.

not only continues to speak, but she also picks up her tongue and throws it at her tormentor. At that point, Julian is blinded in the eye the tongue hits. Julian attempts to disable Christina by removing her tongue, fails, and is himself physically disabled with partial physical blindness by the saint for his previous metaphoric blindness.

These are only brief and selected illustrations of the way disability appears and is narrated in only one genre of medieval literature. The range of depictions of disability in medieval literature is enlightening. It demonstrates the complex understanding of disability as well as the changing perceptions across geographies, time periods, and circumstances. In studying these narratives, we come to see that disability in the Middle Ages did not conform to one, simplistic story. While there certainly were negative approaches at times, there were also positive and neutral ones as well, which humanizes the cultural history of the disabled rather than relegating it to stereotypes.

Diversity Studies

The blockbuster 2018 film *Black Panther* presents an African culture that developed independently of colonialization and the transatlantic slave trade. One of the actresses, Danai Gurira, in reflecting on her role as Wakandan general in the film, makes a powerful observation: "Africans always wonder—'Who would we have been if we weren't colonized?' And she [the character Okoye] protects what we would have been, and to me, it made her very palpable."[18] The fictional world of Wakanda is based loosely on the Mutapa empire of fifteenth-century Zimbabwe as well as other medieval African cultures, such as Mali. For a medievalist, the significance of

---

18 Michel Martin, "Danai Gurira On Her 'Black Panther' Role: 'She Protects What We Would Have Been'," *National Public Radio*, February 17, 2018, https://www.npr.org/2018/02/17/586172340/ danai-gurira-on-her-black-panther-role-she-protects-what-we-would-have-been.

Gurira's statement is the realization that "what might have been" is actually medieval Africa, the continent before European colonizers and slavers disrupted its history and culture. It's a time period when African empires thrived and, for the most part, governed themselves.

Just as there are any number of contemporary works that use the European Middle Ages as inspiration for their settings, *Black Panther* is not the only work of modern fiction to experiment with the idea of a pre- or non-colonial Africa. There is a growing genre of speculative fiction in this genre. At the turn of the twentieth century, Pauline Hopkins wrote *Of One Blood* about the discovery of lost Black kingdoms. In the twenty-first century, Marlon James creates a medieval-esque fictional world in his *Black Leopard Red Wolf* on the scale of J. R. R. Tolkien, but set within the framework of African history and mythology.

Once we make the hypothesis that medieval Africa is a space in which we can imagine the continent and its people without intrusion, the study of this history and culture takes on a different weight. Handed down through oral tradition to griots, African storytellers and the keepers of history, texts like the thirteenth-century *Epic of Sundiata* tell the story of the empire of Mali as it was founded by Sundiata Keita and surrounding countries with its own legendary past.[19] At the time of the founding of Mali, the nobles created its constitution, called the Kurukan Fuga, within which is the Manden Charter. The Charter, inscribed by UNESCO on the list of Intangible Cultural Heritage for Humanity, poetically advocates for "social peace in diversity, the inviolability of the human being, education, the integrity of the motherland, food security, the abolition of slavery by razzia (or raid), and freedom of expression and trade."[20] This document is essential reading to contextualize the values of medieval Africa and the later

---

19 Djibril Tamsir Niane, *Sundiata: An Epic of Old Mali*, trans. G. D. Pickett (Harlow: Longman, 1965).

20 "Manden Charter, proclaimed in Kurukan Fuga," United Nations Educational, Scientific, and Cultural Organization, accessed

rise of transatlantic slavery. These values might not have always been applied in reality by everyone, but the Charter represents an ideal just as, for example, the Declaration of Independence represents an ideal of American life.

Reading the *Epic* and the Manden Charter in conjunction with such works as the fourteenth-century Muslim Moroccan scholar Ibn Battuta's travel writings reveals a complex society with social and trade networks that stretch to Europe and Asia.[21] During Ibn Battuta's travels, the emperor of Mali, which then included Ghana among other neighboring lands, was Mansa Musa, who is considered one of the wealthiest people in history, due in main to the empire's trade in gold and salt. He is represented on the *Catalan Atlas* (ca. 1375), a mappa mundi attributed to Cresque Abraham, a Jewish illuminator. Mansa Musa is depicted sitting on a plush throne with a golden crown and surrounded by the cities of his empire. It is critical to note that he appears as similar in prestige and rank to the European kings on the map.[22]

Similar observations are possible in looking at the art of medieval Africa. The Block Museum of Art at Northwestern University in Illinois, under the direction of Associate Director of Curatorial Affairs Kathleen Bickford Berzoc, presented *Caravans of Gold, Fragments in Time: Art, Culture and Exchange Across Medieval Saharan Africa* in 2019, the first major museum exhibition to highlight the art and culture of medieval Africa in order to rectify its underrecognized impact. In the guide to the exhibition, Berzoc declares:

> *Caravans of Gold, Fragments in Time* shifts the popular narrative of Africa's history—seen predominantly through the lens of the Atlantic slave trade and colonialism—by bringing

---

April 15, 2022, https://ich.unesco.org/en/RL/manden-charter-proclaimed-in-kurukan-fuga-00290.

21 *Ibn Battuta in Black Africa*, trans. and ed. Hamdun and King.

22 For a history of Mali, see Conrad, *Empires of Medieval West Africa*. For discussions of primary medieval African texts, see Fauvelle, *The Golden Rhinoceros*.

forward an earlier history that reveals thriving, far-reaching systems of circulation and exchange in the Sahara, and the central and foundational role they played in global networks of the era. The history, we argue, must be accounted for in understanding the world today.[23]

The exhibition includes many fragments of artifacts, including glass, pottery, and porcelain, as so much of the material history of Africa has been damaged over time, but also textiles, documents, and other objects loaned from Mali, Morocco, and Nigeria. That these objects are loaned through partnerships with African institutions is in itself significant as it speaks to discussions about the ethics of Western museums owning artifacts essentially stolen from other countries, a controversy that is also examined by *Black Panther*.

The field of art history, like other premodern fields, is considering how to be more inclusive and embrace the global Middle Ages. Such exhibitions as *Caravans of Gold* are an example in practice of this initiative. The Material Collective, an organization of medievalists working on visual materials, posted "Ten Proposals for a More Ethical Art History" authored by a student at Elon University, Emily Clark. Clark makes several excellent points about the involvement of students in the professional work of art history—and, by extrapolation, other fields—as well as the need for accessible scholarship, but she especially pinpoints the larger context for studying the global Middle Ages:

> A more ethical art history critiques systems of power with an aim to decolonize the discipline. This calls for emphasizing the importance and necessity of understanding power, identity, and cultural exchange across time and in a global context. It helps students to develop the ability to recognize and articulate engagement with systems of power. Then, language, skills, and problem-solving abilities can be cultivated in order to critique and dismantle those systems.[24]

---

23 *Caravans of Gold*, ed. Berzock, 24.

24 Emily Clark, "Ten Proposals for a More Ethical Art History: An

Including global humanities in the study of the Middle Ages is not about being politically correct or about looking at something pretty from a different culture or even just about being inclusive, as vital as that is. It's about recognizing the ingrained systems of inequality and power imbalance and finding ways to push back against them. Culture in all its forms is evocative.

Undergraduate Perspective," *Material Collective*, June 19 2019, http://thematerialcollective.org/ten-proposals-for-a-more-ethical-art-history/. See also Reilly, *Curatorial Activism*.

CASE STUDIES IN MEDIEVAL LIBERAL ARTS
I. HUMANITIES

"Domestic Abuse Needs No Metaphors"[25]

The mention of domestic abuse in the Middle Ages is often met with skepticism, as if somehow it is a forgone conclusion that abuse was both far more rampant then than it is today and that it was universally perceived as acceptable behavior.

As always, the Middle Ages proves to be far more complex. Marie de France's twelfth-century Anglo-Norman romance *Yonec* provides us with a startlingly stark test case to consider how domestic abuse was understood in the Middle Ages—and how it was condemned.

Locked in a Tower

Yonec begins with a common occurrence in medieval romance: an arranged marriage. Here, between an old, but rich and powerful lord and a beautiful, high-born young lady. The arrangement is described in terms of acquisition and practicality as the elderly lord needs an heir for his vast fortune. Once married, "love" is mentioned on his part at least, but again only in terms of possession and jealousy, to the point that the lord wants to control the lady's body and freedom by keeping her confined:

> Her beauty and sweetness roused his ardor,
> So he planned carefully how to guard her.
> He locked her up in a tower, alone
> In a big room paved with stone [...]
> He kept her there more than seven years—
> They never did engender heirs;
> From that tower she didn't descend
> Not for a relative, not for a friend.[26]

---

25 A companion to: Kisha G. Tracy, "Werewolves as a Metaphor for Domestic Abusers," *The Public Medievalist*, February 21, 2019, https://www.publicmedievalist.com/werewolf-abuse/.

26 Translations are from *Yonec*, trans. Judith Shoaf, University of

Seven years the young bride is locked in this tower, for-bidden from seeing friends and family. She is completely isolated—except for the lord's sister, whose loyalty is to her brother and who controls the lady's movements at the lord's order: "He gave the order, she'd obey." Perhaps most telling for a story of this genre and time period, writ-ten by a Christian writer, the lord will not allow the lady even to go to church, to "hear Mass, do God's works."

This situation is not shrouded in ambiguity or packed in metaphor. It does not require interpretation. A mar-riage is arranged, and the husband imprisons his wife in a tower, preventing her from engaging in any social or reli-gious interaction. These actions are common to abusive relationships. The National Coalition Against Domestic Violence (NCADV) in the United States defines a number of characteristics of psychological abuse, including "con-trolling what the victim can or cannot do," "isolating the victim from friends and/or family," and "denying the victim access to money or other basic resources."[27]

The lord is a domestic abuser.

It might be tempting to dismiss this fact by chalking it up to "those primitive people" in the Middle Ages. But the NCADV reports that "17.9% of women have experienced a situation where an intimate partner tried to keep them from seeing family and friends." Unfortunately, such an individual as the lord would not be out of place in the modern world. Indeed, he would not be unique to any time period. He just happens to have a convenient castle tower.

Effects of Abuse

As a victim of domestic abuse, the lady also is not a uniquely medieval character. Marie de France recounts the effects of this situation, the psychological and physical

---

Florida, 1993, https://people.clas.ufl.edu/jshoaf/files/yonec.pdf.

27 "Facts about Domestic Violence and Psychological Abuse." *National Coalition Against Domestic Violence*, 2015, https://assets.speakcdn.com/assets/2497/domestic_violence_and_psychological_abuse_ncadv.pdf.

trauma, characteristics that would be all too familiar for any victim. She is described as living "in sorrow and pain" and "weeping, sighing, weeping again." These emotions are physically manifested in her appearance:

> She lost her beauty, as a lady would
> Who didn't care if she looked good.

We get very little in the way of description of the lady at the beginning of the story. The characteristics that are highlighted are "noble," "wise," "well-mannered," and "beautiful." It is her beauty that the lord covets. His actions then cause her to lose that beauty. That she "didn't care if she looked good" is an indication of a bleak state of mind, but, even further, it is almost a loss of identity. Carol A. Lambert notes that an impact of psychological abuse is that a victim "experiences a loss of herself or parts of herself, eroding her identity."[28] As one of the main identifiers we have of the lady, her beauty, disappears, is she the same woman we meet at the beginning or has abuse fundamentally changed her?

According to *Abuse: An Encyclopedia of Causes, Consequences, and Treatments*, the "psychological effects of domestic abuse are extensive and pervasive,"[29] and the NCADV reports that "there is a relationship between intimate partner violence and depression and suicidal behavior."[30] In addition to the loss of the lady's beauty, Marie de France makes two references for her desire for death. One as the narrator:

> For herself, the best wish she could make her
> Was for swift death to come soon and take her.

---

28 Carol A. Lambert, "Putting to Rest 'Why Doesn't She Just Leave?," *Psychology Today*, June 12, 2018, https://www.psychologytoday.com/us/blog/mind-games/201806/putting-rest-why-doesnt-she-just-leave.

29 *Abuse: An Encyclopedia of Causes, Consequences, and Treatments*, ed. Rosemarie Skaine (Santa Barbara: ABC–CLIO, 2015), 102.

30 "Statistics," *National Coalition Against Domestic Violence*, accessed April 15, 2022, https://ncadv.org/statistics.

And one in the lady's own words:

> "Alas! I was born on an evil day!
> Hard and cruel is my destiny!
> This tower is a prison for me,
> And only death will set me free."

While she does not indicate that she would take her own life, her desire for death is clear, for she believes that death is preferable to her imprisonment and continued state of existence.

A further effect of the abuse the lady suffers is resentment for those who put her into this position, particularly the family who brokered the arranged marriage. She bitterly wishes for a curse to fall on them:

> A curse on my family
> And on all those, collectively,
> Who gave this jealous man my hand,
> Gave me his body for husband!

As a reader, it is difficult to feel anything other than disgust for the lady's family. There should be a responsibility on the part of a family arranging a marriage for one of its members. The author seems to be commenting on the culpability of knowingly placing, in this case, a woman into an abusive domestic situation. They share the guilt for her suffering.

Meeting Emotional Needs

Contrary to popular belief, medieval romances—rather like their modern counterparts—examine far more than positive intimate relationships. As a genre written primarily for the nobility, they reflect the concerns that were on their audience's minds. For instance, an unmarried lady reading the Lais of Marie de France might be preoccupied with thoughts of a future, looming arranged marriage. What might this husband be like? Will he be good to her? What will happen if he's not?

Yonec explores the worst-case scenario to these questions, but it also provides a fantasy solution. What does a lady trapped in an abusive marriage want? A magical lover to treat her the way she should be treated. The lady articulates this desire, having heard stories of such lovers:

> The sad redeemed, the wronged made right.
> A knight might find a maiden-lover
> Sweet and fair, by thinking of her;
> Ladies could find lovers who
> Were handsome, gentle, valiant, true-

Enter Muldumarec, a shape-shifting knight who flies in hawk form through her window and confirms his devotion and worthiness by taking Mass (magically transforming into her likeness so as not to raise the suspicion of the lord's sister). With the lady's consent, they consummate their relationship, and the knight returns on numerous occasions at her request, treating her with the gentleness and care that she has thus far been denied.

Once the lady's emotional needs start to be met, the physical and psychological toll of her abuse starts to lift:

> Next day she gets up, not at all sick.
> She was so happy all that week.
> She learned she has a precious body,
> And she recovers all her beauty.
> Now she really prefers to exist
> Home alone--other pleasures aren't missed.

The suicidal tendencies wane as she recovers a sense of self-worth, of bodily autonomy, of choice. Her "form and face" are "quite renewed" as her beauty, her identity, returns along with her happiness. Unfortunately, it is these changes that alert the lord to the presence of the shape-shifting lover, allowing him to set the trap that leads to Muldumarec's death—adding murder to the lord's crimes.

"Why Doesn't She Just Leave?"

A ubiquitous, and victim-blaming, question always seems to arise in domestic abuse circumstances: why doesn't she just leave?

When Muldumarec is mortally wounded and leaves the tower, the lady makes the hasty and risky decision to follow him:

> But, with a great cry, she follows.
> She gets out through a window—
> It's a miracle she's not killed below,
> For the wall was twenty feet deep
> Right there where she made her leap.

Why didn't she do this before? Because jumping out of the tower window is dangerous, the narrator telling us that it was a "miracle" that she survived. Perhaps if the abuse continued without any relief, she might have eventually thrown herself from the window to take her own life.

Even had she succeeded in escaping sooner, where would she have gone? We already know that her family placed her in this situation in the first place. It is unlikely they would support her in leaving the husband. She has no friends—the lord has seen to that. She has no resources, no money.

Abuse victims often believe, correctly or incorrectly, that they have no alternatives and no place to go. Lambert notes that the "why doesn't she leave" question is an "erroneous belief that an abused woman has agency—a capacity to exert power—in her relationship, when just the opposite is true." There are any number of reasons why a victim does not leave an abusive relationship. *Women's Aid*, a charity in the United Kingdom working against domestic abuse, cites that "41% (37 of 91) of women killed by a male partner/former partner in England, Wales and Northern Ireland in 2018 had separated or taken steps to separate from them."[31] Leaving means possibly putting your life in even more extreme danger.

Even after Muldumarec dies, the lady does not leave her abusive husband. When she expresses fear that the lord will kill her for the affair, her dying lover gives her a magic ring he teaches her to use that will erase the lord's memory and protect her from being "harassed." At this point, Muldumarec has revealed that she is pregnant, so she also has a child to worry about and care for, which complicates further any decision she might make to leave

---

31 "Why don't women leave abusive relationships?," *Women's Aid*, accessed April 15, 2022, https://www.womensaid.org.uk/infor-mation-support/what-is-domestic-abuse/women-leave/.

the husband. *Women's Aid* lists a fear of being unable to support a child or even having the child taken away as a main reason a woman does not leave an abusive relationship. In this case, even the one person the lady has come to trust is dead.

Medieval Perceptions of Domestic Abuse

So was abuse "acceptable" in the Middle Ages? This story would indicate otherwise.

Through the lady's words, Marie de France tells us that women who took a lover in extenuating circumstances were not "blamed for such affairs." In a story that has obvious Christian values—needing a supernatural figure to take Mass, for instance, in order to prove his belief in God—it allows for adultery, which tends to be frowned upon by Christianity, when domestic abuse is a factor.

Domestic abusers, in any time period of history, are not always punished, but—spoiler alert!—this lord is eventually beheaded for the crime by his own stepson, Yonec, the child of the lady and Muldumarec. The lord's punishment may take a while to come to pass, especially given his power and wealth (factors that have determined legal punishment for crimes for centuries), but it eventually comes in the most poignant and damning of forms.

Domestic abuse happened—as it does now—and it was at times willfully overlooked—as it is now. But it was far from being universally "accepted." It was questioned, condemned, and, yes, punished. No metaphors needed.

Chapter 2

The Middle Ages and STEM

> Not only did they not have the technology that we do now,
> but I assumed that we know a vast amount more than they
> did because of that lack of technology. Although at a first
> glance it may seem true, the idea that those providing the
> information back then, such as historians and scientists,
> were all wrong and did not make advances in their time
> is an unfortunate notion. In each generation, we are gifted
> with many influential persons who bring about changes
> in our current era of the world. Why would it be different
> during the medieval time?
>
> *Anonymous student*

The medieval has a prominent role to play in science, technology, engineering, and mathematics, whether it is in terms
of the historical foundations of study, new discoveries, or the
recognition and understanding of chronological patterns.
The Middle Ages operates before certain major technological inventions and yet individuals exhibit scientific inquiry.
Aspects of STEM existed or are anticipated in this period,
sometimes in sophisticated forms, particularly in the East
although not exclusively so. The Middle Ages is the time of
transfer from oral to written (then to printed) text. This shift
in technology is essential to the study of literature, storytelling, individualism, identity, memory, book production, and so
much more. We require humility in recognizing the achieve-
ments of civilizations before our "tools of progress" made
certain activities comparatively "easy" and second nature.

The very image of technological progress is sometimes misleading. The printing press saved us time; therefore, it is better than handwriting. The internet makes life easier; therefore, it must be better than the time before the internet. This sense of constant updates in technology contributes to the thought that we must be progressing as a species and can mask the connections that motivate the purposes of invention.

Beyond the intellectual origins of STEM that existed in the medieval period, we must recognize the knowledge generated from the period. Modern scientists and mathematicians are more and more looking to the Middle Ages to inform their research questions. Doctors have been reading and testing medieval medical recipes. Epidemiologists, especially in the COVID era, look to medieval pandemics to understand health statistics, including the effect of the Plague outside of Europe.[1] Climatologists mark the patterns in climate change, finding confirmations and contradictions in primary accounts that can help predict future changes. Architects and engineers study medieval cathedrals and other structures to refine and create new designs. Far from being modern-centric, STEM fields have their foundations in the medieval and can return to the medieval to advance their current research.

There is perhaps no more evocative example of these connections than the fire at Notre Dame Cathedral in Paris on April 15, 2019. As the world watched the cathedral in flames, many were convinced there would be nothing left once the fire was contained. To our surprise, when the smoke cleared, while the roof and spire collapsed, the walls were still there. Engineers, architects, and medievalists quickly tried to find out why, concluding that it was the cathedral's medieval

---

[1] For example, see *Pandemic Disease in the Medieval World*, ed. Green. Also see Green, "Plagues Past, Paths Forward." For studies on the Plague in Africa, see the special issue entitled "Sillages de la peste noire en Afrique subsaharienne : une exploration critique du silence / Black Death and its Aftermaths in Sub-Saharan Africa: A Critical Exploration of Silence," *Afriques* (2018), https://journals.openedition.org/afriques/2084.

structure that saved it. Notre Dame was built with the thirteenth-century innovation, flying buttresses. This reinforcement prevented the fire from crumbling the walls.

After the fire, there was much debate about how and if it should be rebuilt. Officials overseeing this decision consulted with the site managers of the experimental archaeology project in northern Burgundy, Guédelon Castle (https://www.guedelon.fr/). Guédelon is being built from scratch using medieval techniques and materials. Over seventy master craftsmen and other artisans, as well as non-skilled volunteers, are working under a scientific committee of experts to build a castle that would have theoretically been constructed beginning in 1228. Their goals include having a "two-way" relationship with scientists, utilizing advice from the modern scientific community and then providing their data and findings back to impact further investigations. These discoveries prove invaluable for the reconstruction of Notre Dame, not to mention other advances in architecture technologies, as stone workers with the experience of those at Guédelon might soon be in high demand.[2] Additionally, Guédelon is active in uncovering medieval practices for green construction and sustainable building with such techniques as "wattle-and-daub or rubble walling, making and using limewashes, traditional terracotta roof tiles, oak shakes, flax and hemp ropes."

Sustainable architectural techniques like these are a part of our intangible cultural heritage. Indeed, UNESCO has officially recognized similar such skills. Techniques used in timber-framed structures such as the Buddhist temple of Horyuji, built in the early 600s in Japan, were added to UNESCO's Intangible Cultural Heritage list in 2020.[3]

---

2 Eleanor Beardsley, "Notre Dame Fire Revives Demand for Skilled Stone Carvers in France," *National Public Radio*, July 20, 2019, https://www.npr.org/2019/07/20/743010875/notre-dame-fire-revives-demand-for-skilled-stone-carvers-in-france.

3 "Building on tradition: Japanese architectural craftsmanship recognized by UNESCO," *The Japan Times*, December 18, 2020, https://

Experiments in sustainable building are far from being the only contribution of the Middle Ages to environmental sciences. Studies in historical climatology have contributed considerable insight into the causes of and trends in climate change.[4] These studies range geographically in the medieval world, from Byzantium and Greenland to South America and Mesoamerica. Researchers working on trash heaps and the end of organized trash management in the sixth-century Byzantine city of Elusa have found evidence that places the collapse of these frontier regions of the Empire a century prior to Islamic conquest, as previously thought, and closer to the Late Antique Little Ice Age. They suggest that this research, published in the *Proceedings of the National Academy of Sciences of the United States of America*, and "its linkage with volcanic eruptions, rapid climate change, and pandemic raises broader concerns regarding the limits of human resilience in the face of environmental catastrophes."[5] The consequences of volcanic eruptions are the emphasis of much historical climatology, especially as eye-witness accounts can also corroborate them. Studies of ice cores in Greenland and Antarctica have revealed that cooling events occurred for up to ten years after large eruptions and potentially confirms that these eruptions were significant causes of "sixth-century pandemics, famines, and socioeconomic disruptions in Eurasia and Mesoamerica."[6]

Five to six hundred years later, centred around 1000–1200, there was another Medieval Climate Anomaly (MCA). Research has more often focused on the impact of this event

---

www.japantimes.co.jp/news/2020/12/18/national/japanese-architectural-craft-unesco-intangible-heritage/.

4 See Lieberman and Gordon, *Climate Change in Human History*.

5 Guy Bar-Oz et al., "Ancient trash mounds unravel urban collapse a century before the end of Byzantine hegemony in the southern Levant," *Proceedings of the National Academy of Sciences of the United States of America* 116, no. 17 (2019): 8239–48 at 8239.

6 M. Sigl et al., "Timing and climate forcing of volcanic eruptions for the past 2,500 years," *Nature* 523 (2015): 543–49 at 543.

in the northern hemisphere, such as that which indicates a period of warmth in Greenland.[7] Newer studies suggest there were corresponding effects in the southern hemisphere, specifically South America. The conclusions suggest that the "most likely key drivers for the medieval climate change are multi-centennial Pacific and Atlantic ocean cycles, probably linked to solar forcing."[8] Solar forcing, or the variation in the amount of solar energy absorbed by the Earth, is one of the effects of massive volcanic eruptions. A transition from the MCA to the Little Ice Age occurred in the early 1300s. Research suggests that the conditions during this time in Europe, named the Dantean Anomaly after Dante Alighieri, have remarkable similarities to the peculiar "seesaw conditions" in the same region in 2018. These rapid transitions could have been partially responsible for the Great Famine and the Plague later in the century.[9] Other studies in central Asia are questioning the belief that the Mongol invasion was solely responsible for the decline of hubs along the Silk Road in the early thirteenth century. Rather, it seems that climate change affecting the confluence of the major rivers, the Amu Darya and Syr Darya, was a direct contributor.[10]

---

7 G. Everett Lasher and Yarrow Axford, "Medieval warmth confirmed at the Norse Eastern Settlement in Greenland," *Geology* 47, no. 3 (2019): 267–70.

8 Sebastian Lüning, Mariusz Gałka, Florencia Paula Bamonte, Felipe García Rodríguez, and Fritz Vahrenholt, "The Medieval Climate Anomaly in South America," *Quaternary International* 508 (2019): 70–87 at 70.

9 Martin Bauch, Thomas Labbé, Annabell Engel, and Patric Seifert, "A prequel to the Dantean Anomaly: the precipitation seesaw and droughts of 1302 to 13017 in Europe," *Climate of the Past* 16, no. 6 (2020): 2343–58, https://doi.org/10.5194/cp-16-2343-2020.

10 Willem H. J. Toonen et al., "A hydromorphic reevaluation of the forgotten river civilizations of Central Asia," *Proceedings of the National Academy of Sciences* 117, no. 52 (2020): 32982–88, https://doi.org/10.1073/pnas.2009553117.

Climate change also has modern impacts on the preservation of medieval archaeology. Modern archaeology is itself dependent upon scientific practices. DNA and isotope analysis of organic deposits can provide insight into the habitations of different settlements and migrations. Cold environments can preserve this material far more effectively; thus, Norse settlements in particular are rich in organic data. The problem, however, is that consistently higher temperatures in Arctic regions is increasing soil temperatures, thus degrading organic content, such as wood and bone. A study on seven archaeological sites in West Greenland suggests that "the effect of future climate change on degradation indicates that 30–70% of the archaeological fraction of organic carbon (OC) could disappear within the next 80 years."[11] The loss of knowledge of the past this represents is devastating.

On a positive note, medieval science and engineering may also help provide solutions to the effects of climate change. In Miraflores and Canchayllo, two communities in the Peruvian Andes, their ecosystem, called *puna*, was drying out due to climate fluctuations. The Mountain Institute, the only international, non-governmental organization to focus on mountain communities and the environmental issues they face, partnered with the local people to restore mostly-forgotten water regulating systems, including silt dams, water reservoirs, and canals, that were built starting in 1000 to increase the amount of available water. This project has been a success and has led to the creation of the award-winning "Ancestral Technologies and Climate Change" initiative by The Mountain Institute, which they are replicating in other areas.[12] Peru has

---

11 Jørgen Hollesen, Henning Matthiesen, Rasmus Fenger-Nielsen, Jakob Abermann, Andreas Westergaard-Nielsen, and Bo Elberling, "Predicting the loss of organic archaeological deposits at a regional scale in Greenland," *Scientific Reports* 9, no. 9097 (2019): https://doi.org/10.1038/s41598-019-45200-4.

12 "Ancestral Technologies and Climate Change," *The Mountain Institute*, accessed April 15, 2022, http://mountain.org/ancestral-technologies-climate-change/. Erica Gies, *Water Always Wins* (Chicago:

also passed laws that created funds, called Mechanismos de Retribucion por Servicios Ecosistemicos (Mechanisms of Reward for Ecosystem Services), to invest in "natural infrastructure," including restoring 1400-year-old techniques still used for water management.[13] A related discovery has been made in Tikal, Guatemala. The Maya built a water filtration system that relied on zeolite and crystalline quartz that purified the local water contaminated with cyanobacteria, allowing the city of Tikal to thrive.[14]

What these examples tell us is that the study of the Middle Ages is very much a part of STEM, and, conversely, STEM fields have much to learn from looking back at the Middle Ages.

Disability Studies

The medical approach to disability studies focuses on diagnosis, which then is often tied to curing or managing impairments. How we see this approach in medieval disability studies varies from medieval understandings of the physical causes, manifestations, and treatments of impairments to modern diagnoses and applications of historical evidence. The former research increases an appreciation for historical medical knowledge and combats the caricature of medieval medicine as exclusively informed by superstition and magic.[15] Indeed, the word "medieval" in modern medical parlance is often used as a disparaging synonym for a reliance on "astrologers" and "vendors of snake oil" (interesting to note that "snake

University of Chicago Press, 2022) explores premodern practices with water. See https://slowwater.world/.

13 Erica Gies, "Why Peru is reviving a pre-Incan technology for water," *BBC Future Planet*, May 18, 2021, https://www.bbc.com/future/article/20210510-perus-urgent-search-for-slow-water/.

14 K. B. Tankersley, N. P. Dunning, C. Carr, et al. "Zeolite water purification at Tikal, an ancient Maya city in Guatemala," *Scientific Reports* 10, no. 18021 (2020): https://doi.org/10.1038/s41598-020-75023-7.

15 See Falk, *The Light Ages*.

oil vendors" are mostly associated with periods later than the Middle Ages).[16] The research indicates the utility and the impact of studying historical bodies and bodies of knowledge.

In 2015, microbiologists tested an Old English eye salve recipe from the ninth-century Bald's *Leechbook* translated by medievalist Dr. Christina Lee.[17] To their great surprise, they found that it was highly effective as an antibiotic against the MRSA bacteria, a treatment-resistant superbug with disabling effects. There is much of interest here. The efficacy of this recipe and others indicates that medieval medical practice was far more than superstition and guesswork. Lee and the other researchers chose this particular recipe because some of the ingredients were already being tested for their medical effectiveness. Their future research will use a similar method in choosing which recipes to test. Considering how many medieval medical recipes exist—Middle Eastern and European, among others—analyzing the ingredients, both in theoretical and experimental environments, could yield countless avenues for research at all levels and potentially yield new modern medicines.

One of the most familiar medieval diseases is leprosy. There is rarely a medieval-based film that does not depict at least one instance of the disease. In some ways, it has almost become synonymous with the period. The modern name for leprosy is Hansen's Disease, and, while it is certainly less prevalent today, around 250,000 people across the world, with the exception of Europe, get the illness each year. Its significance is evidenced by the fact the US Center for Disease Control and Prevention still maintains resources about it (www.cdc.gov/leprosy/index.html). Recent research has indi-

---

16 John Browne, "Technology can propel healthcare out of the Middle Ages," *Financial Times*, June 19, 2019, https://www.ft.com/content/68a65ffa-91c9-11e9-8ff4-699df1c62544.

17 Emma Rayner, "AncientBiotics—a medieval remedy for modern day superbugs?," *The University of Nottingham*, March 30, 2015, https://www.nottingham.ac.uk/news/pressreleases/2015/march/ancientbiotics---a-medieval-remedy-for-modern-day-superbugs.aspx.

cated far more complexity in the pathogens that caused leprosy in the European Middle Ages. Previously, it was believed that only two branches of *Mycobacterium leprae* were the causes of medieval leprosy, but further analysis of medieval genomes indicates that there were a diverse number of branches, some of which are associated with Asia. *M. leprae* strains from different branches have even been found within the same cemetery. These conclusions have implications for the understanding of modern dissemination of the disease.[18]

In one case, in a cemetery for a *leprosarium* (a hospital for lepers), in Winchester, United Kingdom, an eleventh- to twelfth-century pilgrim skeleton has been genotyped as a *M. leprae* strain associated with South-Central and Western Asia. Of further interest in this study is that the facial features of the skull are atypical for northern Europeans. This in addition to analysis of the tooth enamel indicates that the young adult male was certainly not from Winchester, raising questions about the spread of leprosy, especially along pilgrim routes. Further, the researchers can tell that there are only minimal skeletal indicators of leprosy, suggesting that the physical indicators of the disease might not have manifested to a great extent, raising questions about the lived experience of this individual.[19]

Diagnosing leprosy in historical skeletons is relatively uncomplicated given DNA testing. Other conditions are not as straightforward to identify. Medical doctor Þórður Harðarson, in 1984, advanced the theory that the famous Icelandic saga warrior and poet Egill Skallagrímsson had Paget's disease, even suggesting the condition should be renamed in honor

18 Verena J. Schuenemann et al., "Ancient genomes reveal a high diversity of *Mycobacterium leprae* in medieval Europe," *PLOS Pathogens* 14, no. 5 (2018), https://doi.org/10.1371/journal.ppat.1006997.

19 Simon Roffey et al., "Investigation of a Medieval Pilgrim Burial Excavated from the *Leprosarium* of St Mary Magdalen Winchester, UK," *PLOS Neglected Tropical Diseases* 11, no. 1 (2017), https://doi.org/10.1371/journal.pntd.0005186.

of Egill. Paget's disease, first named in the late nineteenth century, is characterized by malformed and hardened bones. Jesse Byock built on this theory in 1993, discussing the interconnections between literary and archaeological evidence to provide support for the diagnosis, including the descriptions of Egill's physical "ugliness" in the saga and his increasing disability as he aged as well as the descriptions of his reinterment a century after his death and the condition of his skull as "scalloped" and unable to be broken.[20] Byock theorizes that the effects of the disease contribute to Egill's status as a great warrior, his inability to fit in completely with his society, and his own perception of himself, thereby helping us to understand better both Icelandic sagas and Icelandic culture.

While the archaeological evidence in the case of Egill is descriptive, we have other physical remains. Paget's disease, while rare in human populations, appears to be prevalent in certain geographical pockets. For instance, in a cemetery at Norton Priory in Cheshire, United Kingdom, dating from the eleventh to the fifteenth centuries, scientists used protein analysis, a relatively new method of diagnosing ancient bones, to confirm Paget's disease in a significant percentage of the skeletons studied. Previously, a few of these skeletons were theorized to have the disease based upon osteological observations only. Some of the individuals are much younger than most modern people who manifest the disease, suggesting a different historical variant. This area in northwest England is known for having a higher percentage of Paget's disease in its population for centuries, the causes for which are still unknown, but studies such as this one in Cheshire might help to illuminate them.[21]

---

20 Jesse Byock, "Skull and Bones in *Egils saga*: A Viking, A Grave, and Paget's Disease," *Viator: Medieval and Renaissance Studies* 24 (1993): 23–50.

21 Kathryn Krakowka, "Picking out Paget's disease using proteomics," *Current Archaeology*, July 4, 2019, https://www.archaeology.co.uk/articles/science-notes-picking-out-pagets-disease-using-proteomics.htm.

In their written findings, the scientists analyzing the Cheshire site advocate for a multidisciplinary approach to such research: "Overall these findings confirm the benefits of a multidisciplinary approach which allows investigation of the wider relationship between leprosy, medieval pilgrimage and *M. leprae* transmission." I would also add disability studies to this list as the researchers do who discovered a thirteenth to sixteenth-century Icelandic woman diagnosed with Facio-Au-riculo-Vertebral sequence. They indicate that this woman probably manifested some disfigurement and other disabili-ties, and they note that such archeological and medical iden-tification "has the potential to contribute to the discussion of disability and perceived disability in the past."[22] As another example, archaeological evidence for ancient and medieval individuals with Down syndrome are scarce due to the diffi-culty of diagnosis from skeletal evidence, although there are significant representations in historical art. The youngest and earliest remains of a child with the syndrome have been iden-tified in Saint-Jean-des-Vignes, in northeastern France. The five- to seven-year-old who lived in the fifth to the sixth cen-tury exhibits many features including particular cranial forma-tions, such as a large cephalic index and a flat occipital bone. In this case, given there is no difference in the burial of this child and the others in the cemetery, the researchers theorize there was no stigma attached to the child during their life.[23]

In these cases and others, scientific diagnosis can be allied with other evidence to demonstrate a more complete image of the lived experience of individuals with disabilities. Studies in osteobiography, the physical narrative of a person as told in their bones, is a perfect example: "Osteobiography

---

22 Sarah Hoffman, Laurie Sadler, Trevor Totman, and Lea Bagne, "A Possible case of Facio-Auriculo-Vertebral sequence (FAVs) in an adult female from medieval Iceland (13th–16th Century)," *International Journal of Paleopathology* 24 (2019): 41–47.

23 Maïté Rivollat et al., "Ancient Down syndrome: An osteological case from Saint-Jean-des-Vignes, northeastern France, from the 5–6th century AD," *International Journal of Paleopathology* 7 (2014): 8–14.

has already proved its value in providing 'a past with faces,' a past in which all people, rather than just textually privileged ones, have humanity and agency rather than remaining 'faceless blobs'."[24] This particular work is just starting to be applied to medieval disability studies.[25]

Diversity Studies

Dawn Bikowski and Talinn Phillips, in *Teaching with a Global Perspective*, state:

> Faculty in the humanities or social sciences often find it straightforward to implement GLOs [global learning outcomes], while in STEM courses, GLOs might ask students from diverse background to interact and learn from each other, for instructors (including international teaching assistants) and students to communicate authentically, and for students to develop an identity as a member of the scientific community.[26]

Such a statement implies that the humanities and the social sciences are expected to teach diversity studies content while STEM fields can only influence certain habits of mind. This inference is incorrect. All fields should be and can be involved in both engaging diversity content and influencing habits as is exemplified by the study of the Middle Ages.

The history of science should not overlook the Middle Ages as it does so frequently and inexplicably and, more specifically, should not overlook the influence of medieval Islam, which also encompasses the expertise of a large

---

24 John Robb et al., "Osteobiography: The History of the Body as Real Bottom-Line History," *Bioarchaeology International* 3, no. 1 (2019): 16–31 at 18.

25 Jenna Dittmar and Bram Mulder presented their team's work on "Reconstructing Physical Impairment in Medieval Society: A Biomechanical Approach" at the 2019 European Association of Archaeologists conference.

26 Bikowski and Phillips, *Teaching with a Global Perspective*, 89.

area.[27] The scientific advancements and discoveries of medieval Islam drew on the knowledge of all the lands they conquered, expanded into, and contacted, from Spain, Europe, Byzantium, and North Africa to Persia, China, and India, then returned that influence. Through such major intellectual and translation centres as Gondeshapur in Persia, captured in 638 and containing a community of exiled Nestorian Christians, Greek texts in particular became a central source of scientific knowledge and, as they were translated on a large scale into Arabic, the starting point for Islamic innovations. This interest also saved and transmitted Greek texts that could have been lost to time. In terms of diversity studies, it is significant to note the multicultural nature of Islamic sciences and, in particular, that those who contributed to it were also of many ethnicities. Ibn Khaldun in his fourteenth-century *Muqaddimah*, although perhaps exaggerating, acknowledges that "most Muslim scholars both in the religious and in the intellectual sciences have been non-Arabs."[28] Arabs, Jews, Christians, Persians, Africans, among others, not to mention societies such as the Greeks and Babylonians, were all jointly involved in the development of Islamic science.

To discuss all of the discoveries by medieval Islam, even just during the Golden Age, the eighth to the fourteenth centuries, takes far more space than we have here. I will mention briefly a few in order to illustrate the breadth of fields in which these peoples were interested. In mathematics, scholars, "clarifying the intellectual legacy of the past, putting it in workable order, and then enriching it with significant innovation," were in particular interested in perfecting and applying Greek geometry and Hindu arithmetic, and they originated algebra and algorithm.[29] Indeed, the critical number zero developed its significance in India before crossing to North

27 See Nasr, *Science and Civilization in Islam* and Turner, *Science in Medieval Islam*.

28 Ibn Khaldun, *The Muqaddimah*, chap. 6, §42.

29 Turner, *Science in Medieval Islam*, 43–47.

Africa and then finding its way to Europe in the thirteenth century.[30] In geography and astronomy, they built massive observatories, helmed by renowned teachers, in a number of the major Islamic cities from Baghdad to Toledo, refining or inventing a number of instruments such as the astrolabe (invented by the Greeks), the quadrant, and the compass (invented by the Chinese).[31] In optics, the scientist Alhazen alone contributed to the study of spherical and parabolical mirrors, refraction, and atmospheric phenomena in addition to the physiology of the eye and principles of vision.[32] These brief examples do not include the previously-mentioned advancements in medicine and natural sciences as well as astrology and alchemy, among other disciplines.

As the Middle Ages contributed to the history of knowledge, modern STEM fields contribute to our understanding of human history. In early 2018, the Natural History Museum of London announced new information concerning Cheddar Man, a ten-thousand-year-old Mesolithic skeleton discovered in the early twentieth century in Somerset. DNA evidence proves that Cheddar Man has the genetic markers for darker-pigmented skin, closer to that found in sub-Saharan Africa. This discovery indicates that European populations at that time had much darker skin than originally believed.[33] The announcement of the story told by Cheddar Man's DNA was met with considerable disbelief by white supremacists who promote the idea of Europe as an historically Caucasian space from the beginning of its history.

Human remains, found in Sidon, Lebanon, near a castle, have been identified as Crusaders killed in battle during the thirteenth century. DNA testing indicates that this group of Cru-

---

30 See Amir D. Aczel, *Finding Zero: A Mathematician's Odyssey to Uncover the Origins of Numbers* (New York: St. Martin's, 2015).

31 Nasr, *Science and Civilization in Islam*, 80–88.

32 Nasr, *Science and Civilization in Islam*, 128–30.

33 Kerry Lotzof, "Cheddar Man: Mesolithic Britain's Blue-Eyed Boy," *Natural History Museum London*, April 18, 2018, https://www.nhm.ac.uk/discover/cheddar-man-mesolithic-britain-blue-eyed-boy.html.

saders was a far more diversely-mixed group than anticipated. These individuals were Europeans, people from Western Asia, and mixed individuals that showed similar genetic makeup to groups living in Northern Spain or Basque territories.[34] Such conclusions indicate that "there's more to learn about who the Crusaders were and their interactions with the populations they encountered."[35] A similar conclusion can be drawn from other studies, like one looking at the DNA of early seventh-century Alemannic skeletons found in Niederstotzingen, Germany. The grave goods found with these remains indicate a diverse group of Frankish, Lombard, and Byzantine origin. The DNA confirmed this diversity, demonstrating a mixture of northern, eastern, and central European with eastern Mediterranean. The researchers conclude that "at least in death, diverse cultural affiliations could be appropriated even within the same family across just two generations."[36] Another study indicates that women in fifth to sixth-century Bavaria demonstrate a higher-level of diversity than men of the same period. Most interesting were skeletons with deliberately-elongated skulls, which "were very genetically diverse, demonstrating a wide range of both modern northern/central and southern/southeastern European ancestry, and even some samples with East Asian ancestry."[37] As for Vikings, who are so often touted

---

34 Marc Haber et al., "A Transient Pulse of Genetic Admixture from the Crusaders in the Near East Identified from Ancient Genome Sequences," *The American Journal of Human Genetics* 104 (2019): 977–84.

35 "A History of the Crusades, as Told by Crusaders' DNA," *phys.org*, April 18, 2019, https://phys.org/news/2019-04-history-crusades-told-crusaders-dna.html.

36 Niall O'Sullivan et al., "Ancient genome-wide analyses infer kinship structure in an Early Medieval Alemannic graveyard," *Science Advances* 4, no. 9 (2018), https://doi.org/10.1126/sciadv.aao1262.

37 Krishna R. Veeramah et al., "Population genomic analysis of elongated skulls reveals extensive female-biased immigration in Early Medieval Bavaria," *Proceedings of the National Academy of Sciences of the United States of America* 115, no. 13 (2018): 3494–99.

as "white," a study of 442 Viking-age skeletons from across Europe and Greenland revealed high levels of non-Scandinavian ancestry, particularly from southern Europe and Asia, providing evidence for a multi-cultural genetic history.[38]

Despite such insights, DNA studies are fraught with more than just proving their scientific validity. Researchers presenting their evidence need to be aware of the potential implications of their conclusions. Susanne Hakenbeck cautions, for instance, that unnuanced genetic research may unwittingly support ethnic divides.[39] Even sophisticated studies may find their work oversimplified and used for "pernicious arguments about race and ethnicity."[40]

Beyond ethnic diversity, scientific studies are also confirming diversity in gender roles. Chaco Canyon in northwestern New Mexico was home to a Puebloan people from approximately 800 to 1200 who were known for producing "corrugated ware" pottery. Based upon modern studies of the culture's descendants as well as, frankly, gender assumptions about the division of labor, it has been generally accepted that this pottery was created by women. A recent study, however, took a look at the average size of thumbprints left in the pottery. To their surprise, these studies indicate that the fingerprints were evenly-distributed among the genders. Even more surprising, the older the pottery the higher the percentage of male-sized fingerprints. If these findings are corroborated, the assumptions about gender division of labor need to be reevaluated.[41]

---

38 Ashot Margaryan et al. "Population Genomics of the Viking World," *Nature* 585 (2020): 390–96, https://doi.org/10.1038/s41586-020-2688-8.

39 Susanne E. Hakenbeck, "Genetics, archaeology and the far right: an unholy Trinity," *World Archaeology* 51, no. 4 (2019): 517–27, https://doi.org/10.1080/00438243.2019.1617189.

40 Megan Gannon, "When Ancient DNA Gets Politicized," *Smithsonian Magazine*, July 12, 2019, https://www.smithsonianmag.com/history/when-ancient-dna-gets-politicized-180972639.

41 John Kanter, David McKinney, Michele Pierson, and Shaza

A similarly assumption-changing discovery was made concerning a well-known Viking grave in Birka, Sweden. Since its excavation in 1878, it has been believed to be the body of a male only because it appeared to be such a standard example of a Viking warrior of high status—thus, must be male. Osteological and DNA evidence, however, revealed that the warrior was indeed a female, challenging the idea of warriors as male-only. Despite the fact that the Viking warrior woman, such as shield-maidens and Valkyries, has been a favorite figure for generations, there was massive pushback against the researchers after their findings were published. To such an extent that they had to publish even further evidence and extensive source studies to support and validate their conclusions.[42] This type of misidentification is not unheard of—reflect, for instance, on the fact that the bones being potentially considered as those of famous aviatrix Amelia Earhart were indeed originally discovered in 1940 and were dismissed as Earhart's solely on the basis that they were too "manly" to be those of a high-society woman!

As a further example of science calling into question assumed gender divisions, the discovery of lapis lazuli in the teeth of an eleventh or twelfth-century German nun confirms growing assertions by scholars that women were far more involved in book production than previously credited. By happenstance, a separate study of the dental calculus of this forty-five to sixty-year-old woman revealed the rare substance of lapis lazuli. It is known that the pigment was used in illuminations and that artists would lick their brushes repeatedly during the process of creating them, thus explaining the presence of the mineral in the nun's teeth and provid-

Wester, "Reconstructing sexual divisions of labor from fingerprints on Ancestral Puebloan pottery," *Proceedings of the National Academy of Sciences of the United States of America* 116, no. 25 (2019): 12220–25.

42 Neil Price et al., "Viking warrior women? Reassessing Birka chamber grave Bj.581," *Antiquity* 93, no. 367 (2019): 181–98.

ing potential physical evidence of the often-hidden work of women in literary production.[43]

It is important to remember that bones cannot tell us everything about the lived experience of the human beings they once were. With what gender did these individuals identify? Were there other categories of gender recognized in these societies? While the skeletons may not give us this information, it helps illuminate the questions. STEM fields are uniquely situated to provide material evidence to question singular narratives and bring to light the diversity of the Middle Ages.

---

43 A. Radini et al., "Medieval women's early involvement in manuscript production suggested by lapis lazuli identification in dental calculus," *Science Advances* 5, no. 1 (2019), https://doi.org/10.1126/sciadv.aau7126.

CASE STUDIES IN MEDIEVAL LIBERAL ARTS
2. STEM

"A Modern Look at Medieval Remedies"

Did you know that modern microbiologists have recently started testing medieval medical recipes? That one made of garlic and onion has tested as highly effective against the MRSA bacteria, long known as treatment-resistant? Did you know that scientists have proven there is truth to the story about soil in Northern Ireland that was believed by early peoples, including Druids, to have medicinal qualities? At first glance, these all might sound improbable, but I assure you they are real.

First, a look at the space in which natural remedies were often found: gardens. Gardens were a common presence in the Middle Ages and still found at many medieval heritage sites not to mention in the popular *Brother Cadfael* series. They were egalitarian; even if they might take different forms, they could be found at the peasant's house and the lady's manor. The layout and purpose of gardens was a point of much contentious discussion.

Santa Clara University installed, in 2003, a garden in memoria of St. Clare of Assisi (ca. 1193–1253). Rather than being a strict reconstruction of any one garden, "Saint Clare" is an amalgam of medieval research, particularly that of the thirteenth-century Albertus Magnus, imaginative interpretation of St. Clare's stages of life, and modern horticulture. It exemplifies Albertus' description:

> There are, however, some places of no great utility or fruitfulness but designed for pleasure [...] They are in fact mainly designed for the delight of two senses, namely sight and smell [...] Behind the lawn there may be great diversity of medicinal and scented herbs, not only to delight the sense of smell by their perfume but to refresh the sight with the variety of their flowers, and to cause admiration at their many forms in those who look at them.[44]

---

44 Harvey, *Mediaeval Gardens*, 6.

The layout of Saint Clare's is indicative of the multiplicity of roles the medieval garden served with its five main groupings: wild flowers, medicinal and household, lavender, kitchen, and spiritual. Gardens were created for their aesthetic and religious purposes, yet, they also simultaneously served practical medicinal or culinary purposes.

There was a certain amount of concern about the manipulation of the natural world that gardens represented. As an illustration, in the fourteenth-century Middle English romance *Sir Orfeo*, a retelling of the Greek Orpheus myth, the queen Heurodis lounges in her garden:

> Thus this queen, Dame Heurodis
> Took two maidens of refinement
> And went in late morning
> To play by an orchard
> To see the flowers spread and spring
> And to hear the birds sing.
> They sat them down all three
> Under a fair ympe-tree,
> And well soon this fair queen
> Fell asleep upon the green. (ll. 63–72)[45]

The ympe-tree in this passage seems to be selected on purpose. It is a grafted tree, the process of joining different species of plants together—a technique we might call a "Frankenstein," which illustrates the concerns about unnaturalness. That the queen falls asleep under such a tree in her carefully-cultivated garden and then immediately experiences a life-disrupting dream in which the king of fairies eventually kidnaps her alludes to the problematic nature of the space.

Indeed, gardens were not always safe spaces for far less abstract reasons. As exemplified by the Poison Garden currently at Blarney Castle in Ireland, there are a number of plants that are toxic. It was just as important, if not more so, to recognize these plants as those

---

45 Translation is mine, from the Middle English *Sir Orfeo*, in *The Middle English Breton Lays*, ed. Anne Laskaya and Eve Salisbury (Kalamazoo: Medieval Institute Publications, 1995).

that could be safely eaten. Spanish Jewish philosopher Mosheh ben Maimon, known as Maimonides, identifies many of these plants in his *On Poisons and the Protection against Lethal Drugs* (ca. 1199). In several cases, he names the remedy if a poisonous plant is ingested, whether by accident or malicious design:

> It is easy to assassinate someone with hemlock and henbane. When a person knows that this is the case (i.e. that he has been poisoned by one of these), he should hasten to take [some] bark of the mulberry tree, boil that in vinegar, and first induce vomiting with that and then with milk.[46]

What is particularly interesting here is that the poison and the remedy are both plants that could be found in or near a medieval garden. Healers and killers growing next to each other.

The types of healing plants one might find in a medieval garden varied, particularly depending upon geography and climate. There are a few that tend to show up regularly, such as rosemary, chamomile, and sage. Rosemary, as the fourteenth-century *Zibaldone da Canal* by a Venetian merchant illustrates, was considered a bit of a panacea, protecting against an impressive list of complaints from worms to rheum to nightmares.[47] Chamomile, for instance as noted in the fifteenth-century English manuscript Ferguson 147 (in Glasgow University Library), is associated with menstruation and virginity. Sage, according to the *Tacuinum Sanitatis*, originally an eleventh-century Arabic medical treatise that was later translated into Latin, alleviates paralysis and calms the nerves.[48] Several herbals of different time periods and origin provide us with details about the uses of plants

---

46 Maimonides, *On Poisons and the Protection against Lethal Drugs*, trans. Bos, 59.

47 *Merchant Culture in Fourteenth-Century Venice: The Zibaldone da Canal*, ed. and trans. John Dotson (Binghamton: Medieval and Renaissance Texts and Studies, 1994), 149–51.

48 Luisa Cogliati Arano, *The Medieval Health Handbook: Tacuinum*

as remedies. For more information, check out the Herbal History Research Network, the DigiVatLib Herbals, and the University of Alcalá Medical Manuscripts.

The work of two modern fields of study has emerged to take a look at the medical knowledge of past peoples, particularly of natural remedies, in order to determine if they have any modern applications. The first field is ancientbiotics, which looks for older remedies to modern ailments. The second is archaeobotany, which analyzes and interprets plant remains found at archaeological sites. Over the last few years, experts in these fields have made remarkable discoveries. The following is just a survey of some of the findings this research has produced.

The most significant contribution by medieval ancientbiotics and the one that brought the field to the public's attention is the work of an interdisciplinary group of researchers, including medievalist Christina Lee, who discovered that a recipe in the tenth-century Old English *Bald's Leechbook* is actually effective against MRSA, a "superbug" resistant to modern antibiotics. The recipe, for a "wen" in the eye, says to "crush garlic and a second *Allium* species (whose translation into modern English is ambiguous), combine these with wine and oxgall (bovine bile), and leave the mixture to stand in a brass or bronze vessel for 9 days and nights." It was proven in the course of the study that the brass or bronze vessel was the determining factor, indicating that the method is as important as the ingredients. The research group is planning on testing other recipes in the book to determine if they have similar applications. A parallel study by Nigerian scientist Mansurah Abdulazeez is being conducted on the anticancer properties of endemic African plants that have been used for generations by traditional healers.[49]

Sanitatis, trans. Oscar Ratti and Adele Westbrook (New York: Braziller, 1976).

49 "Nigerian scientist develops cancer drugs from African plants," *The Guardian (Nigeria)*, August 29, 2019, https://guardian.ng/features/science/nigerian-scientist-develops-cancer-drugs-from-african-plants.

Researchers associated with the Institute for the Preservation of Medical Traditions, which is dedicated to researching ancient knowledge to create new medicines, began work on the medical artifacts found in a Tuscan shipwreck from around 130 BCE. Partnering with geneticists, they found DNA in tablets prepared by the physicians of ancient Greece from the wreckage that included: carrot (panacea), radish, celery, wild onion, oak, cabbage, alfalfa, and yarrow (staunched the flow of blood from wounds), hibiscus extract (probably from east Asia or the lands of present-day India or Ethiopia). While this is not a medieval discovery as such, recipes from Greece greatly influenced medieval remedies.

Twelfth-century German Benedictine St. Hildegard von Bingen, in addition to being everything from an abbess, writer, and composer to a mystic and visionary, is also considered the founder of scientific natural history in Germany. In her *Physica* and *Causae et curae*, she makes around 437 claims of health benefits from 175 different plants. Scholars have started to test out the efficacy of these claims, which have so far turned out to be quite significant. Given that, other researchers have been working to confirm whether the number of correct claims was knowledge or luck. Bernhard Uehleke and her colleagues conclude:

> The hypothesis that Hildegard could have achieved her "correct" claims by chance is to be clearly rejected on the basis of the highly significant level of our new statistical procedure. The finding from this approach that medieval medical claims are significantly correlated with modern herbal indications supports the importance of traditional medicinal systems as an empirical source.[50]

In layman's terms, Hildegard—and by extension other medieval people—knew what she was talking about.

---

50 Bernhard Uehleke, Werner Hopfenmueller, Rainer Stange and Reinhard Saller, "Are the Correct Herbal Claims by Hildegard von Bingen Only Lucky Strikes? A New Statistical Approach," *Forschende Komplementärmedizin* 19, no. 4 (2012): 187–90.

The fifteenth-century Middle English *Lylye of Medicynes* by Bernard of Gordon found in the Bodleian Library (Oxford) manuscript Ashmole 1505 includes approximately 360 recipes with over three thousand ingredients for the treatment of 113 different conditions. Erin Connelly, who has translated the book, and collaborators datamined the text to reveal patterns in ingredient choices to see if they might exhibit medically-useful activity. The takeaway of the research so far is that the remedies do demonstrate effective medicinal properties.[51] Interestingly, the work revealed that language causes complications in this type of research; for example, the herb fennel is referred to as "fenel, feniculi, feniculum, marathri, maratri, and maratrum." Not an easy task to track all the names down.

Stories about the healing powers of particular patches of soil in Boho, Northern Ireland, have circulated for centuries. Druids built an amphitheater in the location because of this reputation. Locals used and still use the soil to treat all kinds of infections, including toothaches. Researchers, after testing the soil, found that indeed it does have medicinal properties and is effective against multiresistant ESKAPE pathogens.[52]

After analyzing the dental calculus, the result of dental plaque mineralization that is found in a number of historical human remains, of an adult male from approximately the ninth to the tenth centuries in the Balearic Islands of Spain, researchers discovered evidence of fern spores. This particular fern, *Asplenium trichomanes*, has been recorded in historical and modern documents as a cure for kidney stones and alopecia. Since it was found in the teeth and is not known as a culinary plant, the

---

51 Erin Connelly, Charo I. del Genio, and Freya Harrison, "Datamining a Medieval Medical Text Reveals Patterns in Ingredient Choice That Reflect Biological Activity against Infectious Agents," *mBio* 11, no. 1 (2018), https://doi.org/10.1128/mBio.03136-19.

52 Luciana Terra et al., "A Novel Alkaliphilic *Streptomyces* Inhibits ESKAPE Pathogens," *Frontiers in Microbiology* 9 (2018): 2458, https://doi.org/10.3389/fmicb.2018.02458.

researchers conclude that it was used for medicinal purposes of this nature.[53]

Given the concerns in the last several years that either we are not discovering as effective of medicines or our modern medicines, especially antibiotics, are no longer as effective as they used to be, there is a distinct need to try out new methods—or, in this case, return to old methods and explore their validity. The number of historical remedies that have been determined to have promising effects, of which these are only a sample, is providing ample proof that looking to the past, particularly the medieval one, is significant for the health of our future.

---

53 Elena Fiorin, Llorenç Sáez, and Assumpció Malgosa, "Ferns as healing plants in medieval Mallorca, Spain? Evidence from human dental calculus," *International Journal of Osteoarchaeology* 29 (2019): 82–90.

Chapter 3

The Middle Ages and the Social Sciences

For over two centuries, American slaveholders, the Knights of the Ku Klux Klan, Nazi Germany, and today's white supremacist self-styled "alt-right" have all promoted a twisted idea of the Middle Ages that props up their white-supremacist fantasies. And unfortunately, their view of the Middle Ages has trickled into the groundwater of the broader popular historical consciousness.

Paul B. Sturtevant, "Race, Racism, and the Middle Ages:
Tearing Down the 'Whites Only' Medieval World,"
The Public Medievalist, February 7, 2017

In light of recent white supremacist and pro-Western civilization events and rhetoric across the United States, the connection between the Middle Ages and the social sciences is more important than ever. Containing disciplines that focus on how humans interact, the social sciences give us insight into multiple aspects of society. Although the history of social science is generally thought to begin in the Age of Enlightenment, the issues it studies and its methodologies are timeless and universal. A resurgence of the use of the Middle Ages to "justify" white nationalism, racism, ableism, misogyny— and any number of other -isms—in American culture can be addressed through the social sciences: sociology, political science, geography, education, economics, among other disciplines. Medieval social scientists explode popular beliefs, such as "there were no people of color in the Middle Ages and therefore they should not be included in fantasy-based video games," which is a matter of representation, or "there were no positive social views of the disabled in the Middle Ages."

A surprising number of popular misconceptions about the Middle Ages feed modern social dynamics, which was tragically on display at the Charlottesville "Unite the Right" rally in 2017 and the January 6, 2021 attack on the United States Capitol building. Confusing misinterpretations of the term "medieval" leads to charged rhetoric that perpetuates misinterpretations and conflict.

On one hand, the term "medieval" is used as a pejorative adjective, deployed when an author or speaker wants to imply "primitive" or "barbaric." So, for instance, articles about the increased spread of diseases among the homeless were published in 2019 in such venues as *The Atlantic*, *Forbes*, *healthline*, and *wbur* that labeled typhus and tuberculosis as "medieval." Even a cursory examination of the history of these diseases reveals that the first reliable mention of typhus is from the late fifteenth century, the very end of the Middle Ages. Tuberculosis has been identified in prehistoric and ancient remains, and there is no specific medieval link with it. Indeed, the best-known outbreak of tuberculosis is from the nineteenth and early twentieth centuries. Yet, the governor of California called this a "medieval" outbreak as did an infectious disease specialist at the Vanderbilt University School of Medicine.[1] Both expressed incredulity at the appearance of these diseases in 2019. While acknowledging the seriousness of these outbreaks, I would express incredulity at the use of the term "medieval" to describe them.

Why is this derogatory view of the Middle Ages so common? The answer has far less to do with the real Middle Ages and far

---

[1] Anna Gorman and Kaiser Health News, "Medieval Diseases Are Infecting California's Homeless," *The Atlantic*, March 8, 2019, https://www.theatlantic.com/health/archive/2019/03/typhus-tuberculosis-medieval-diseases-spreading-homeless/584380/. Brian Mastroianni, "Outbreaks of 'Medieval' Diseases Are Becoming More Common in Cities," *healthline*, April 2, 2019, https://www.healthline.com/health-news/why-medieval-diseases-are-hitting-cities-hard.

more to do with our own need to distance ourselves from the negative aspects of humanity—and a misguided sense, reinforced by the Enlightenment, that "modern" equates to "progress" and anything from the past is "stagnant" or "ignorant." Why do medieval-based television shows and films depict so much rape? Because it is easier to handle the idea that "those" people did that, that it is not something we do anymore. It is easier to believe that we have progressed beyond certain behaviors rather than confronting the reality of what we as humans are collectively capable. It is far more comfortable to label something like rape as "medieval" rather than deal with the fact that one out of every six American women are likely to be victims of rape or sexual assault at some point in their lives.

The opposite view, the idolizing of the "medieval," or what is perceived as medieval, comes with its own issues as this view can lead to or reinforce ideologies like white supremacism and misogyny. Take, for instance, the medieval-related word "chivalry." It is commonly-used today and typically intended to have positive connotations or a lament for its demise.[2] In the Middle Ages, the term referred to the complex understanding of knighthood or the conduct of a knight—in battle, in relationships, in everyday life—that was neither necessarily positive or negative. In more modern times, since approximately the nineteenth century, it has been reduced to a synonym for honorable or brave behavior, particularly of "gallant gentlemen," as noted by the Oxford English Dictionary, towards women, loosely associated with the image of the "knight in shining armor." This over-simplification and misunderstanding of the original term create a space for the glorification of toxic masculinity and the demeaning of women.

An assignment from a class at Shallowater High School near Lubbock in Texas, received criticism (and was eventually removed) for requiring female students to follow the medieval "Rules of Chivalry," including a dress code, "obeying any reasonable request of a male," "never criticizing a male," "addressing all men respectfully by title, with a lowered

---

2 See Utz, *Medievalism: A Manifesto*.

head," and "not showing intellectual superiority if it would offend the men around them."[3] Even more disturbing, it was encouraged that this behavior be carried over outside of school. Purportedly this assignment intended to demonstrate how the "code of chivalry and standards set in the medieval concept of courtly love carries over into the modern day." After reviewing the assignment, experts around the world determined that it bears little resemblance to medieval chivalry of any kind. If the assignment teaches anything, it is only a much more recent misconstruction of the idea.

Describing any time period as "perfect" or a "golden age" ignores the problems that exist in any era, and dismissing any time period as "dark" condemns its contributions to obscurity. Humans are capable of great things, and we are capable of terrible things. If we don't acknowledge both, we are incapable of learning and experiencing true progress.

The COVID-19 coronavirus pandemic (from SARS-COV-2) starkly demonstrates the need for examining and perhaps even predicting human behavior over time. Anthea Hartig, the Elizabeth MacMillan Director of the National Museum of American History, commented that, in the COVID moment, we didn't experience history repeating itself, but rather the "folds of time: where do the sides start touching?"[4] Certainly the folds of time start to align when we think about the Plague of the fourteenth century and COVID. There are comparisons in how governments prepared for the potential number of dead, in burial grounds, hospitals, or morgues. Medieval people understood as much as we do now that distance from

---

3 Elisha Fieldstadt, "Texas school scraps chivalry assignment that had girls 'obey any reasonable request of a male'," *NBC News*, March 5, 2021, https://www.nbcnews.com/news/us-news/texas-school-scraps-chivalry-assignment-had-girls-obey-any-reasonable-n1259730.

4 David Smith, "'People see how relevant history is': Smithsonian tackles Covid challenge," *The Guardian*, December 31, 2020, https://www.theguardian.com/culture/2020/dec/31/anthea-hartig-interview-smithsonian-national-museum-of-american-history-covid.

the infected is essential in stalling the spread of disease, and there are accounts of people social distancing and, more radically, leaving cities for isolated areas.[5] Christiane Gruber has characterized Islamic talismanic shirts, inked with Qur'anic verses to protect the body they covered, as a premodern version of personal protective equipment.[6]

Human nature reacts to crises in different ways. Winston Black, in an episode of *The Medieval Podcast*, remarks that "the best use for looking at the Black Death [...] where its value lies is we can see what humanity does in the face of half of the population dying [...] Here is where we see the amazing resilience of medieval people [...] We see people pick up the pieces."[7] We can see the parallels in COVID resilience: essential workers continuing to work (although also similarities in the exploitation of the working class), technology developing to cope with the crisis, medicine and health procedures addressing the spread, families and friends caring for each other. Humans rise to the moment.

Unfortunately, humans also can be simultaneously weighed down by the moment. Literary texts such as Boccaccio's *Decameron* focus on the devastation of the Plague, on the social and economic unrest. More serious, there were isolated incidents of the blaming of vulnerable populations such as Jews for the outbreaks, creating parallels to anti-Asian hatred during COVID. There is unfortunately a "long tradition of hatred" when it comes to finding someone or something to blame for extreme crises.[8]

---

5 See the webinar from the Medieval Academy of America, "The Mother of All Pandemics."

6 Christiane Gruber, "The Arts of Protection and Healing in Islam: Talismanic Shirts as Premodern 'PPE'," *Ajam Media Collective*, April 30, 2021, https://ajammc.com/2021/04/30/premodern-ppe-talismanic-shirts/.

7 Danièle Cybulskie and Winston Black, "The Black Death and COVID-19," *The Medieval Podcast*, March 2020, https://www.medievalists.net/2020/03/black-death-covid-19/.

8 Joanne Lu, "Why Pandemics Give Birth to Hatred: From Bubonic

By examining social issues over time and geography, we can understand our behaviors and motivations and perhaps better learn how to interact with each other.

Disability Studies

The social approach to disability focuses on identifying or mitigating social factors, such as attitudes and resources, which turn impairment into disability as well as the roles the disabled play in society and how society represents the disabled. Museums are ideal locations to study the social approach to disability as they both reflect the histories and issues that are significant to their societies as well as attempt to shape those priorities through education.[9]

Richard III was king of England from 1483 to 1485 when he was killed at the Battle of Bosworth Field in the War of the Roses. His death marked the end of the Plantagenet line and the beginning of the Tudor line. Richard's body was lost after the battle, rather deliberately, and not recovered until 2012, during an excavation of a carpark on the site of the former Greyfriars Priory near Leicester Cathedral. How the remains were identified is a feat of various sciences, including radiocarbon dating, forensic reconstruction of the skull, and mitochondrial DNA comparison with his descendants. Within the margin for error at the nexus of these sciences, the skeleton is Richard. He was reinterred in Leicester Cathedral in 2015.

The King Richard III Visitor Centre was built in 2014 on the site of the discovery. The museum, along with historical information about Richard, his controversial reign, and his death, contains a glass-covered look at the dig site and an

---

Plague to COVID-19," *National Public Radio*, March 26, 2021, https://www.npr.org/sections/goatsandsoda/2021/03/26/980480882/why-pandemics-give-birth-to-hate-from-black-death-to-covid-19.

9 A 2019 proposal, that has caused controversy, before the International Council of Museums seeks to alter the very definition of museums by adding in language about contributing "to human dignity and social justice, global equality and planetary wellbeing."

exhibition dedicated to Richard's body, including one of his most oft-described physical characteristics: his scoliosis. In addition to the other evidence of Richard's identity, one of the first visible markers was the curvature of the skeleton's spine, and the museum presents a reproduction to highlight the distinct bone formation.

Richard III's disability has been re(mis)interpreted for generations, starting shortly after his death and appropriated in metaphor into the present day. When the Tudors took over, they were invested in discrediting their predecessors in order to strengthen their own claim to the throne. Sir Thomas More, a staunch advocate of the Tudors, wrote *The History of Richard III* around 1513–1518, approximately thirty years after Richard's death. The *History*, which does not present Richard in a positive light, places a significant emphasis on the king's physical appearance, implying a connection between that and his apparently flawed character:

> Richard, the third son, of whom we now treat, was in wit and courage equal with either of them, in body and prowess far under them both: little of stature, ill featured of limbs, crooked-backed, his left shoulder much higher than his right, hard-favored in appearance, and such as is in the case of lords called warlike, in other men called otherwise. He was malicious, wrathful, envious, and from before his birth, ever perverse.[10]

More's work was one of the primary sources for Shakespeare's *Richard III* in which the king, depicted as a malicious character, is called a "bunchback'd toad" (Act I, Scene 3). The character of Richard himself, in his first speech opening the play, describes his various physical characteristics as "deformed, unfinish'd," directly linking his disability and what he defines as his resulting deficiencies with his decision to "prove a villain" (Act I, Scene 1). Much has been written about

---

10 Thomas More, *The History of King Richard III*, The Center for Thomas More Studies, accessed April 15, 2022, https://thomasmorestudies org/wp-content/uploads/2020/08/Richard.pdf.

the productions of the play that visually make this link with Richard's hunchback over-emphasized. It is Shakespeare's representation that has survived to modern day, reinforcing the persistent image of the "evil disabled."

The King Richard III Visitor Centre directly engages with the ramifications of this representation. One of the first panels reads:

> Some modern leaders, like U.S. President Franklin D. Roosevelt, have kept their physical conditions private for fear it would make them seem weak. For Richard, it may not have been an issue. Only after death was his body shape given significance as a sign that he was "evil."[11]

This panel begins with the note, "We now know Richard had scoliosis. This may have impacted on his life, but it was evidently not disabling." What this statement conveys to the museum visitors is at a minimum two-fold. First, it indicates that representation of Richard's disability since his death may have been over-exaggerated for a number of (biased) reasons. Second, and more importantly, even with the physical symptoms of scoliosis, the condition did not prevent Richard from becoming a political and military leader, thus not disabling him in the social sense.[12] A later label reinforces this idea by clarifying that Richard's scoliosis "would have put some pressure on his lungs, but clearly did not stop him having an active life." Punctuating this assertion, the beginning panel ends with the reminder (or admonition): "However we judge Richard's actions, his body shape did not reflect his character." In this statement, we see the uncoupling of Richard's disability from his behavior, attempting to undo the image that has accompanied the king for centuries, and by extension has reinforced stereotypes about disability.

---

11 All references to the Visitor Centre exhibits were accurate as of August 2016.

12 For a discussion of kingship and disability see also Beth Tovey, "Kingly Impairments in Anglo-Saxon Literature: God's Curse and God's Blessing," in *Disability in the Middle Ages*, ed. Eyler, 135–48.

A label accompanying the reproduction of the king's spine ends: "Scoliosis is fairly common, affecting 1–3% of the population, including many visitors to this exhibition." One of the clear interpretative goals of this museum is the social stigma of disability. Not only does the exhibition address the representations of Richard's specific disability, it also addresses the stigma of disability, specifically scoliosis, by recognizing the common experience of those who have the condition, even going so far as to point out that visitors to the museum itself are likely to have some degree of scoliosis. Making such a connection seeks to de-stigmatize the idea of disability and, at the same time, creates a link to past individuals, like Richard, who also experienced disability.

The representation of disability in museums, both in the artifacts and in the interpretations, such as labels and guides, reveals the place in history of disabled people and affects how the disabled are viewed and treated.

Diversity Studies

A particularly heinous event occurred in Charlottesville, Virginia, on August 11 and 12, 2017: the Unite the Right rally. There are many reasons to abhor what happened there, not the least of which was the murder of Heather Heyer and the injuring of many others. For medievalists, it became a wake-up call. Photos of white supremacists carrying various types of medieval imagery—shields, Deus Vult crosses, heraldry— flooded our news feeds. While many of us were certainly aware of the appropriation and misuse of the medieval before this event, "Charlottesville" forced us to evaluate exactly how serious the ramifications of this appropriation truly are.

If Charlottesville was a wake-up call, the 2021 attack on the Capitol building in Washington, DC, was a tragic reinforcement of that call. Once again, medieval and medieval-esque representations abounded, displayed next to an array of hate symbols. Prominent among these were the horned helmet and tattoos of Jacob Anthony Chansley, known as the "Q Shaman." Photos of Chansley displayed his tattooed Thor's hammer, the Valknut, and the World Tree all over the news and social media. The Medieval Academy of America's public statement after the assault condemned the "presence of pseudo-medieval symbols and costumes among the rioters in the Capitol" and "reminded us once again of the particular responsibility we have as medievalists."[13] Scholars of color, such as Mary Rambaran-Olm among others, have been sounding the warning about these dangerous appropriations for a long time, and we need to heed them.

The story of Derek Black discussed later emphasizes just how much the medieval appears in white supremacist ideology, not only in the United States but in multiple countries.[14] The Ku Klux Klan call themselves the American Knights, and the name of their newspaper is *The Crusader*. This imagery was also common in Nazi Germany, with typical pictures such as Hitler depicted in armor, as were arguments about race attributed to the Middle Ages, which were in reality eighteenth- and nineteenth-century inventions.

---

13 "MAA Public Statement on the Assault on the U.S. Capitol," *The Medieval Academy Blog*, January 13, 2021, http://www.themedievalacademyblog.org/maa-public-statement-on-the-assault-on-the-u-s-capitol/. See also Matthew Gabriele, "Vikings, Crusaders, Confederates: Misunderstood Historical Imagery at the January 6 Capitol Insurrection," *Perspectives on History*, January 12, 2021, https://www.historians.org/publications-and-directories/perspectives-on-history/january-2021/vikings-crusaders-confederates-misunderstood-historical-imagery-at-the-january-6-capitol-insurrection and Richard Fahey, "Marauders in the US Capitol: Alt-right Viking Wannabes & Weaponized Medievalism," *University of Notre Dame Medieval Studies Research Blog*, January 15, 2021, http://sites.nd.edu/manuscript-studies/2021/01/15/marauders-in-the-capitol-alt-right-viking-wannabes-weaponized-medievalism-in-american-white-nationalism/.

14 See, for instance, Paulo Pachá, "Why the Brazilian Far Right Loves the European Middle Ages," *Pacific Standard*, March 12, 2019, https://psmag.com/ideas/why-the-brazilian-far-right-is-obsessed-with-the-crusades.

These views are based on a belief that the Middle Ages existed only in Europe and an all-white Europe in which men were essentially allowed to do whatever they wanted. The number of rallies being organized that promote both "Western civilization" with "straight pride" and "anti-immigration" speaks volumes about the prevalence of these beliefs, not to mention such movements as the America First Caucus, which announced its existence by supporting "Anglo-Saxon political traditions," a code for extreme "whites only" beliefs that gained popularity in the late nineteenth and early twentieth centuries.[15] University of Oxford lecturer Rachel Moss laments the popular view of the Middle Ages as the "mainstream perception of the Middle Ages remains one of a white, Christian world: a *Game of Thrones* universe without dragons but with just as much rape."[16] These obviously erroneous and limited interpretations of this period in history are echoed in conventional misunderstandings that gets perpetuated through repetition and media representations.

Games of Thrones is a prime example of the perpetuation of misrepresentations of the medieval in television and film. The medieval-esque world is presented with almost no people of color, and those that do exist in this fictional world are represented with distinct overtones of "barbarism," merely as cannon fodder, or as peoples in need of saving. The reaction to protests about the show are often met with the counterargument that "people of color did not exist in the Middle Ages." Setting aside the illogic of a fantasy narrative having to conform to any supposed realities, this argument has been disproven repeatedly by experts in the field.[17] The organiza-

---

15 Adam Serwer, "'Anglo-Saxon' Is What You Say When 'Whites Only' Is Too Inclusive," *The Atlantic*, April 20, 2021, https://www.theatlantic.com/ideas/archive/2021/04/anglo-saxon-what-you-say-when-whites-only-too-inclusive/618646/.

16 "The long view: scholars assess the state of history," *Times Higher Education,* February 15, 2018, https://www.timeshighereducation.com/features/long-view-scholars-assess-state-history.

17 See *The Public Medievalist* "Race, Racism and the Middle Ages"

tion MedievalPOC (www.patreon.com/medievalpoc) provides multiple resources to correct this image, and African-American intellectuals have been emphasizing medieval multiculturalism at least since the mid-1800s with modern scholars continuing the work.[18] And yet it is an argument that persists. For instance, at the announcement that a Black actress might be cast as Maid Marian in a Robin Hood film, there was outrage at what was deemed to be completely inauthentic. Even the casting of Idris Elba as Heimdall in the Marvel Thor films, which for the record are not historically accurate portrayals of either medieval Scandinavia or the fictional Asgard, caused serious amounts of "righteous" indignation.[19]

It isn't only fictional representations that cause such visceral pushback. When the DNA evidence about the Cheddar Man came out, revealing his darker skin pigmentation, the reactions were just as fierce. One such response, among others collected in an article in *Vice*, speculates, "No showers back then, maybe he was just a bit dirty."[20] Even seemingly

---

series as well as Heng, *The Invention of Race in the European Middle Ages*, the special issue of *postmedieval* edited by Whitaker, "Making Race Matter in the Middle Ages," among other work by Kavita Mudan Finn, Dorothy Kim, David Perry, and many others. Also see articles by Geraldine Heng, Anthony Bale, and Roland Betancourt in Kristen Collins and Bryan C. Keene, "Scholars Respond to an Exhibition about Medieval Prejudice," *The Getty Iris*, March 6, 2019, https://blogs.getty.edu/iris/scholars-respond-to-an-exhibition-about-medieval-prejudice. For a bibliography, see Hsy and Orlemanski, "Race and medieval studies: a partial bibliography."

18 See Matthew Vernon, "Whose Middle Ages? Remembering Early African-American Efforts to Claim the Past," *The Public Medievalist*, October 23, 2018, https://www.publicmedievalist.com/whose-middle-ages.

19 See Helen Young, "White-Washing the 'Real' Middle Ages in Popular Media," in *Whose Middle Ages? Teachable Moments for an Ill-Used Past*, ed. Andrew Albin et al. (New York: Fordham University Press, 2019), 233–42.

20 https://www.vice.com/en/article/gy8gqm/how-daily-mail-readers-are-reacting-to-the-fact-an-early-brit-was-black.

innocuous uses of language in media reinforce these ideas. An article that came out in *Newsweek* was titled "Ancient Chess Piece with Islamic Designs Discovered in Norway, Baffling Archaeologists."[1] The use of the word "baffling" is itself baffling, for the bulk of medievalists would not be surprised to find evidence of such an interaction between medieval cultures.

There are number of ways to demonstrate the reality of diversity of ethnicities in the Middle Ages. The very idea of a global Middle Ages helps to alter the assumption that all things medieval are only European. By expanding our scope of the medieval into all continents of the world, we automatically include the presence of all peoples, not just those who are European or white. Also, by looking at the world as a whole, we can explore how cultures met and interacted with each other. This could be through trade, such as the Silk Road or in the Mediterranean. As has been argued many times, it would be impossible, for instance, for Europe to have gold and salt without contact with Africa or silks without contact with China.[2] Then there is the study of the composition of Europe itself, which was never the exclusive white "safe space" that white supremacists would like to believe.

To demonstrate this latter point, I will focus only on one of any number of examples, but this particular one I have viewed in person and has significant modern ramifications. The Black Madonna tradition in art works, such as paintings and statues, originated in the Middle Ages around the twelfth to the fifteenth centuries, concentrated in France but also in other areas; approximately four to five hundred are known in Europe. In a study of around one hundred examples, Leonard Moss divided them into three categories with the majority falling into the first of "dark brown or black madonnas with

---

1 Sydney Pereira, "Ancient Chess Piece with Islamic Designs Discovered in Norway, Baffling Archaeologists," *Newsweek*, January 29, 2018, https://www.newsweek.com/ancient-chess-knight-norway-islamic-arabian-archaeologists-793897.

2 See Fauvelle, *The Golden Rhinoceros*; Kurlansky, *Salt*; and Liu, *The Silk Road in World History*.

physiognomy and skin pigmentation matching that of the indigenous population."[3]

The prominence of the tradition is attributed to the stories of miracles surrounding these works of art. The Black Madonna of Czestochowa, Poland was said to have originally been painted by St. Luke then brought to Poland via Constantinople in 1384. More likely, it was a sixth- to ninth-century piece. The original was destroyed beyond repair by robbers in 1430. It is credited with a number of miracles, including several Polish military victories, making the painting a national monument.[4] The medieval prominence of the Black Madonna is still alive today. For instance, the Czestochowa Madonna was the model for the Black Madonna, Our Lady of Jasna Gora, a 1938 painting now housed in Saint John the Guardian of Our Lady Parish in Clinton, Massachusetts. It has also become an image used by especially Black artists, in exhibitions such as Steven Greenfield's 2020 "Black Madonna," Theaster Gates' 2018 "Black Madonna," and Harmonia Rosales' 2018 "New World Consciousness" and 2020 "Miss Education: Reclaiming Our Identity."[5]

3 Michael Duricy, "Black Madonnas: Origin, History, Controversy," *All About Mary*, University of Dayton, accessed April 15, 2022, https://udayton.edu/imri/mary/b/black-madonnas-origin-history-controversy.php.

4 Michael Duricy, "Czestochowa Black Madonna," *All About Mary*, University of Dayton, accessed April 15, 2022, https://udayton.edu/imri/mary/c/czestochowa-black-madonna.php.

5 Greenfield, *Black Madonna*; "Theaster Gates: Black Madonna," Kunstmuseum Basel, September 6 to October 21, 2018, accessed April 15, 2022, https://kunstmuseumbasel.ch/en/exhibitions/2018/gates; "Harmonia Rosales | Miss Education: Reclaiming Our Identity," Museum of Contemporary African Diasporan Arts, March 11 to May 24, 2020, accessed April 15, 2022, https://mocada.org/harmonia-rosales-miss-education-reclaiming-our-identity/. See Lexi Manatakis, "Harmonia Rosales repaints classic artworks to show God is a black woman," *Dazed*, September 5, 2018, https://www.dazeddigital.com/art-photography/article/41202/1/harmonia-rosales-repaints-classic-artworks-god-is-a-black-woman-rjd-gallery.

Several years ago, I visited the Black Madonna in Chartres Cathedral, which is a 1508 wooden replica of a thirteenth-century silver version. The dark-skinned statue was clothed in brilliant golden raiment, and there were a constant stream of visitors paying homage and snapping photos of her. A few years after I visited, I was shocked to run across a current photo of the Madonna. I hesitated to believe that she was the same statue I had seen. After a "restoration" in 2017, the Black Madonna is now white, a decision that has caused controversy for visitors, and pilgrims, who expect to see the black visage. The Chartres Madonna is by far not the only one to be "cleaned." The thirteenth-century Black Madonna in Magdeburg Cathedral in Germany underwent cleaning in the nineteenth century. The statue is still billed as the "Black Madonna" in the visitor's guide, but many, like myself, have a hard time finding it given its now pale white appearance.

The Black Madonna tradition speaks to the presence of people of color in the European Middle Ages just as their white-washing, literally, in modern times speaks to the problematic issues with race we experience today. In many ways, these statues and paintings are metaphors for the misunderstanding and misrepresentation of diversity in the Middle Ages not to mention they are artifacts of social erasure.

CASE STUDIES IN MEDIEVAL LIBERAL ARTS
3. SOCIAL SCIENCES

"Myth-Busting Medieval Disability"

Many widespread myths about disability have unfavorable effects on the social perception and treatment of people with disabilities. There are even more myths about medieval disability, and these have a way of prompting inaccurate beliefs about the heritage of people with disabilities.

Let's explore five of the most pervasive.

Myth #1: Disability, especially mental health, is a modern concept.

Truth: Disability is a universal human experience, across all time periods and geographies.

In medieval Christian Europe, there was an underlying understanding that we are all in essence disabled due to original sin. From a religious standpoint, there was really no "normal," here on earth at least, against which to compare. More practically, medieval people were well aware that the "able" body could become "disabled" at any time, through accident, warfare, disease, etc., making the line a very thin, permeable one. Although probably not intentionally, George R. R. Martin's medieval-esque world of *Game of Thrones* illustrates this philosophy well in that characters move between these states frequently.

What has changed? One major difference is language. Today, we have a considerable amount of medical terminology for states of ability, physical and mental. In the Middle Ages, terminology varied by time period and geography, and, along with it, so did social conceptions. The Society for the Study of Disability in the Middle Ages has created an open access source, the Medieval Disability Glossary (https://medievaldisabilityglossary.hcommons.org/), with the stated mission to demonstrate "the complexity of early writers' approaches to disability" as "the vocabulary of impairment plays a vital role in shaping the identities of individuals and communities." Taking one random entry from the glossary: the term "barren," the inability to bear children, is derived from the Old French *baraine*, and related terms include *unfructuous* and *unfruitful* in Middle English, *unberende* and *unwæst-meberende* in Old English, and *sterilis* in Latin. These are only examples from four languages out of the vast array throughout the Middle Ages, and each word has different connotations and usages, complicating yet invigorating examination of this concept.

Such studies shed light on the changing linguistic practices surrounding disability. Words that were once commonplace receive later scrutiny. For instance, the word "mad" used to be a medical diagnosis handed down by physicians, yet today that word would rarely be used by doctors.

The words we use today, while helpful in some ways, also serve to categorize and label, sometimes to the detriment of individuals, especially when social stigma accompanies the labels. It is useful to look to the pre-modern era, a time period before current medical and legal terminology and definitions dominated and shaped (mis)perceptions. One of the benefits of studying medieval disability is that the terminology and descriptions must be explored, examined, their etymology traced. It eliminates some of the social "baggage" that comes with certain labels, allowing for the study of people with disabilities on their own terms in their own contexts.

Myth #2: Effective disability accommodations, technologies, and treatments are a modern advancement.
Truth: Human beings have been innovating accommodations, technologies, and treatments for disabilities throughout our history.

In the thirteenth-century French manuscript in the British Library, Royal 10 E IV, of the *Decretals* of Gregory IX, there is an illustration on fol. 110r of what appears to be a blind beggar holding a staff and the end of a leash around the neck of a large dog that is walking in front of him. In a thirteenth-century Chinese scroll titled "Spring on the Yellow River" in the Metropolitan Museum of Art and the print held by the Perkins School for the Blind, a man with a staff holds the leash of a dog leading him through a busy street. These are only two examples of illustrations depicting a long history of guide dogs.[6]

Humans are, on the whole, incredibly innovative. Accommodations were common to assist those with disabilities to participate fully in life. Eyeglasses as we know them were invented at least by the thirteenth century. Crutches and other assistive mobility devices appear in numerous manuscript images, being used by everyone from knights to peasants. Various forms of prosthesis were invented, usually on a case-by-case basis. One of the most sensational finds was in a sixth to eighth-century Italian grave. Archaeologists found a man with a knife they believe to have been used as a prosthesis for an amputated right fore-arm.[7]

Keep in mind that people with disabilities today still regularly fight for necessary accommodations.

Myth #3: People with disabilities were always viewed and treated negatively, especially in the Middle Ages.
Truth: It's complicated.

Modern people often incorrectly view the Middle Ages as monolithic in its beliefs, whether in religious ways or the incorrect yet persistent flat-earth theory. In this case, there is a wide-spread idea that medieval people viewed disability with distaste and skepticism, perceiving it only as manifestations of evil or sin. The reality is, as always, far more complex.

The real issue with the myth is the "ALWAYS viewed and treated negatively." In any time period, including the modern era, there is rarely anything that applies to everyone everywhere. Yes, sometimes people with disabilities were viewed and treated negatively in the Middle Ages—just as

---

6 See Krista Murchison, "Guide Dogs in Medieval Art and Writing," *Dr. Krista A. Murchison*, accessed April 15, 2022, https://kristamurchison.com/medieval-guide-dogs/.

7 Ileana Micarelli et al., "Survival to amputation in pre-antibiotic era: a case study from a Longobard necropolis (6th–8th centuries AD)," *Journal of Anthropological Sciences* 96 (2018): 1–16.

now. But, equally, people with disabilities were viewed and treated positively or neutrally—just as now.

Let's take a look at the Glossary's entry on "leprosy." Popular perception, aided and abetted by cinematic representations, would have it that leprosy was only considered a condition to be shunned and castigated in the Middle Ages. Certainly, that happened. In a four-teenth-century Middle English sermon, it is used as a metaphor for lechery, equating the condition of the soul to the leprous body. Yet, if we stopped there, considered this the definitive representation, we would not learn all of the story. A fifteenth-century Middle English sermon depicts a leper as the means of spiritual blessing, ending with the leper ascending into heaven.[8] Even two texts in the same language, of the same genre, written within a century of each other have two different views.

We have medieval accounts of people with mental health issues being bound and incarcerated. Even today, there are instances of both illegal and legal restraining of individuals against their will. Completed in France at the beginning of the fourteenth century, the British Library manuscript Yates Thompson 8 depicts the children's game Blind Man's Bluff, which performs the beating up and mocking of a blind person. Yet, even with these examples of violence and discrimination, we also have others such as the stained-glass windows at Canterbury Cathedral in England that depict St. Thomas Becket mir-aculously healing Hugh of Jervaulx among other individ-uals with various disabilities and diseases.[9] Today Geel in Belgium, a town with a long history of veneration of St. Dymphna, patron saint of mental illness and myriad other illnesses, has created a shared living program, inviting people with disabilities into their homes and families.[10]

---

8 Julie Orlemanski, "Leprosy," *Medieval Disability Glossary*, accessed April 15, 2022, https://medievaldisabilityglossary.hcommons.org/leprosy/.

9 Cheryl Preston, "The Miracles at Canterbury," *The Getty Iris*, July 25, 2018, https://blogs.getty.edu/iris/the-miracles-at-canterbury/.

10 Jackie L. Goldstein and Marc M. L. Godemont, "The Legend and Lessons of Geel, Belgium: A 1500-Year-Old Legend, a 21st-

In excavations in York, they found a skeleton known as the Coppergate Woman. Upon examination, they discovered that this woman had hip dysplasia and likely used a crutch through a significant part of her life. The Jorvik Viking Centre emphasizes that the woman's burial circumstances reveal no special or lesser treatment.[11]

When we consider the entirety of the Middle Ages and all of its geographies, we can imagine the number of different social perceptions that existed—comparable to the range that exists in the modern day.

Myth #4: People with disabilities were always poor and never allowed in positions of power.

Truth: People with disabilities are and have been a part of every aspect of society.

Quite often, when medieval people with disabilities are included as examples in museum exhibitions or other spaces, they are all too often included only as "charity cases" or of the "lower class." See, for instance, the otherwise excellent Getty Museum's "Outcasts: Prejudice and Persecution in the Medieval World," which included a section on "Ableism and Classism" that included the role of disability in charity.[12] What this type of representation unwittingly reinforces is the idea that those with disabilities were prevented from participating fully in all aspects of society, particularly in positions of power.

This is untrue. We have many examples of medieval rulers or people in other positions of power who either

---

Century Model," *Community Mental Health Journal* 39, no. 5 (2003): 441–58 and Lorraine Krall McCrary, "Geel's Family Care Tradition: Care, Communities, and the Social Inclusion of Persons with Disabilities," *Journal of Literary and Cultural Disability Studies* 11, no. 3 (2017): 285–301.

11 "The People of Jorvik," *JORVIK Viking Centre*, accessed April 15, 2022, https://www.jorvikvikingcentre.co.uk/the-vikings/the-people-of-jorvik/.

12 "Outcasts: Prejudice and Persecution in the Medieval World," *The Getty*, accessed April 15, 2022, https://getty.edu/visit/cal/events/ev_1883.html.

clearly had a disability or exhibited signs of disability. In many of these cases, this fact did not interfere with their ability to rule—either physically or in the minds of those they governed.

To name a few rulers: Alfred the Great of Wessex (reigning in various capacities from 871 to 899) had what might have been Crohn's disease and its accompanying chronic pain.[13] Baldwin IV, king of Jerusalem (r. 1174–1185), was known as the "Leper King" as he managed leprosy for most of his life yet there seems to have been no real concern about his ability to rule other than the need to secure a successor.[14] In thirteenth-century Mali, Sundiata Keita began his life unable to walk and became the founder of the Malian empire. Richard III of England (r. 1483–1485) experienced scoliosis, and the connection between his disability and fitness to rule did not begin until after the Middle Ages with a Tudor propaganda campaign against his line, partly supported by Shakespeare's *Richard III*.

While disability at times became a convenient excuse for those who wished to depose a ruler or cast reservations on an individual's right to power, it was not a universal disqualifier.

Myth #5: We can't know the lived experience of medieval people with disabilities.
Truth: We can interpret.

While the man with a knife-hand prosthesis is fascinating unto itself, what is perhaps even more so is the evidence of the wear on the man's teeth as they were used repeatedly to help bind the straps of the prosthesis. Such physical evidence invites us to think about the lived experience of this individual—and others with disabilities. Rosemarie Garland-Thomson has described disability as the "history of our encounters between flesh and world written on our bodies."[15] In this case, the daily need to

---

13 G. Craig, "Alfred the Great: A Diagnosis," *Journal of the Royal Society of Medicine* 84 (1991): 303–5.

14 See Hamilton, *The Leper King and His Heirs*.

15 From a virtual discussion on September 25, 2020, "The Preserv-

manage a prosthetic left signs on this man's skeleton that we can interpret.

It is true that we do not have the advantage of being able to speak directly to people in the Middle Ages, but we can examine literature, legal texts, manuscript images, art, archaeological finds, clothing remains, etc., in order to piece together images of how people with disabilities lived in the Middle Ages and how different geographies and time periods interacted with disability.

If we listen, especially to marginalized or vulnerable populations, past and present, we can learn a great deal.

---

ation of Disability" hosted by Columbia University Graduate School of Architecture, Planning and Preservation.

Chapter 4

The Significance of Studying the Middle Ages

> The fifth responsibility of the student is for the student in pursuit of the sciences to not leave a single aspect of the study of the praiseworthy sciences or any branch of them without giving them careful consideration, in order to apprise himself of its significance and purpose.
>
> *Al-Ghazâlî (ca. 1058–1111, Persia), "The Book of Knowledge,"*
> *Iḥyā' 'Ulūm al-Dīn [The Revival of the Religious Sciences][1]*

Derek Black was the heir-apparent to the hate group *Storm-front* that was founded by his father. Growing up, he had been exposed regularly to a version of medieval history propagated by white supremacists. He was drawn to the period, even making his own armor and participating in medieval reenactment groups. Homeschooled for primary and secondary school, Derek then attended a liberal arts college in Florida, especially to study medieval history. Once there, his preconceptions were challenged regularly inside and outside of the classroom. Finally, he had to confront his beliefs:

> [Derek Black] had chosen New College because he wanted to study medieval history, and he had been drawn to medieval history in part because the mythology of white nation-

---

[1] Al-Ghazâlî, *Iḥyā' 'Ulūm al-Dīn*, trans. Honerkamp, 148. For the sake of clarity and continuity, despite the use of other dating systems by the cultures discussed, all dates provided are based on the Gregorian calendar.

alism centered on the Middle Ages [...] Instead the facts of history pointed him to another conclusion: the iconic European warriors so often celebrated on Stormfront had never thought of themselves as white, Derek decided. Some of them had considered skin color not a hard biological fact but a condition that could change over time based on culture, diet, and climate. They had fought not for their race but for religion, culture, power, and money, just like every other empire of the Middle Ages [...] And if he had been that wrong about history—his field of expertise—then he was also willing to believe he had been wrong about so much else.[2]

At that point, Derek Black left *Stormfront*, turned his back on his legacy of white supremacy, sought to redress the wrongs he had committed, and embraced a different life as a graduate student of medieval studies.

While there were multiple factors in Derek's conversion, his liberal arts education played a crucial role. From the types of classes to the diversity of other students that such colleges attract, the liberal arts experience helped Derek think critically about the fallacies of the "truth" he had been exposed to all of his life. In particular, the study of the heritage and culture of the real Middle Ages opened his eyes to a new way of thinking.

Derek Black's story may be unique, but it demonstrates the power of both the liberal arts, inside and outside of formal education, and the study of the Middle Ages, especially when they are allied together. This book has been conceived to capture the heart of that power.

Significance of Studying the Middle Ages: A Liberal Arts-Style Intervention

For skeptics of the significance of studying the Middle Ages, I would ask that you engage in the following process in order to explore the roots of as well as the validity of your skepticism. This progression of activities and reflection has been

---

2 Saslow, *Rising Out of Hatred*, 241–43.

proven in a formal study of college-level students in general education courses to increase the abilities of individuals, who are in the majority skeptics at the beginning, to articulate the significance of studying the medieval period. For those who are already converts to the unique benefits of studying the Middle Ages, I recommend engaging in this process as well to refine your thoughts.

Examine Initial Thoughts

Ask yourself a version of this question: "As of right now, do you believe that studying the Middle Ages is significant? Why or why not?" As with almost any question, it is the "why" that is the most important here. What beliefs do you have about the study of the Middle Ages? If you do not believe the study is significant, what prevents you from doing so? If you do believe it is, why specifically?

Explore Public Scholarship[3]

I could also call this step: talk and/or listen to the experts. As a student at a university or college, you certainly have one at the front of the classroom, but don't stop there. Look for others with different opinions. There are many ways these days to seek out these experts from the comfort of your living room, especially with the growing number of medievalists who participate in public scholarship. The work of medieval studies is not confined to academic journal articles and books. The study of the Middle Ages is significant beyond the assumed "ivory tower."

This book was designed to be a form of extended public scholarship. The "Studies in the Medieval Liberal Arts" sections are all examples of public scholarship in practice.

---

3 See *Envisioning Public Scholarship for Our Time*, ed. Adrianna Kezar, Yianna Drivales, and Joseph A. Kitchen (Sterling: Stylus, 2018) and *The Humanities and Public Life*, ed. Peter Brooks (New York: Fordham University Press, 2014).

The Public Medievalist is an online magazine (https://www.publicmedievalist.com/) that provides accessible, edited scholarship written by people with expertise for the general public. In addition to individual articles, especially on topics of current interest, they have series on race/racism as well as gender/sexism. Also, several US-based newspapers and magazines, such as *Forbes* and *Pacific Standard,* are looking more and more to medievalists to comment on current events. As with any source, take a look at the credentials of the authors.

If you are inclined to social media, there are innumerable experts at the click of a "follow." On Twitter, there is a thriving community of medievalists. By following #medievaltwitter, you can witness or participate in the development of research ideas, the creation of collaborations, and, yes, the controversies in the field in real time.[4] You will see a number of posts highlighted in this volume.

On Facebook, there are several groups, both academic and popular, for those interested in the Middle Ages. I created the Significance of Studying the Middle Ages Facebook group (https://www.facebook.com/groups/939478049471496/) in order to provide a space for academics, instructors, students, and the general public together to share resources and discuss ideas about why we study the Middle Ages. Since its creation and without too much advertisement, it has grown to over thirteen hundred members, which indicates the level of interest in the period.

Question Preconceptions

Novice students of the Middle Ages often fall back on thinking that the medieval era was "primitive" or "backward," believing that the modern era has progressed far beyond what they see in premodern artifacts. It is part of a tendency—for all of us—to see time periods and people in those time periods as "all" one way or another. It is important to identify and acknowledge these preconceptions.

---

4 See Graham, "What I Learned on Medieval Twitter."

In order to open up conversations about this topic, I developed an activity that I call "Medieval or Modern?" I collected—with the help of social media—a number of quotations, some from modern sources and others from medieval sources. The goal was to find modern quotations, particularly related to gender and ethnicity, that could sound "medieval" and medieval quotations that could sound "modern." In addition, I included more "traditional" sounding quotations from both periods. I heavily edited the quotations to disguise any obvious clues, but the meanings were all retained. Almost universally, students express surprise at the difficulty in identifying the time period of each statement, and they are more willing to discuss their own misconceptions of periodization and the concept of "progress."[5]

As a further note, when I have used this activity in conference presentations to experts in the field, they too have similar experiences as undergraduates. They express difficulty in identifying the time period of the quotations, often commenting that many of them really could be either "modern" or "medieval." Rather than breaking down pre- or mis-conceptions as it does with students, this activity helps experts in the field grapple with how to present our studies and how to discuss the significance of the Middle Ages, especially to wider audiences.

To replicate a portion of this experience, I recommend taking a look at the news on any given day. Ask yourself if the quotations or sound bytes in truth "sound modern," defining for yourself what "modern" means. Or read a collection of medieval texts recommended by an expert and ask yourself if they indeed "sound medieval" and ask what "medieval" actually means.

Confront Prejudices

After the Charlottesville riots in August 2017, medievalists all over the world struggled with how to address the medieval

---

5 Kisha G. Tracy, "Medieval or Modern?," *Medieval Higher Ed*, accessed April 15, 2022, https://medievalhighered.omeka.net/items/show/2.

imagery and information (mis)used by white supremacists and the (mis)appropriation of our field. I felt a moral obligation at that time to educate my students on this misuse. To that end, Fitchburg State librarian Renée Fratantonio and I teamed up to develop an activity that would combine content with information literacy and approach this appropriation through the lens of disinformation, misinformation, and propaganda.

To develop this activity, I sifted through a variety of digital artifacts—web sites, discussion boards, Tweets, memes, historical documents, etc.—that appropriate medieval imagery or themes in order to compile an archive for my students to examine. They look at themed sets of these artifacts with the purpose of identifying main messages and assumptions as well as questions raised.[6]

This activity has proven to be incredibly powerful. Students are often not prepared for the serious application of medieval studies. Discussion in class demonstrates this surprise and concern over the appropriation of medieval imagery, and they begin to ask penetrating questions about the reasons for this appropriation and how the imagery has been distorted and how it can be addressed.

I should warn anyone that this is distressing and triggering material. I do not recommend diving into the internet to access this material. I have provided the link to this activity in the footnote, and the artifacts are only provided through screenshots, not direct links. I also recommend engaging with public scholarship and breaking down preconceptions before you address such ideas as (mis)appropriation. After this stage, move on to the next one of deep research in order to think further about the reality of the Middle Ages rather than the appropriated fantasies.

---

6 Kisha G. Tracy and Renée Fratantonio, "(Mis)Appropriation of the Middle Ages," *Medieval Higher Ed*, accessed April 15, 2022, https://medievalhighered.omeka.net/items/show/35.

Do the Deep Research

At this point, you have likely developed more questions than answers, which is exactly where you should be. Take those questions, and research them. Dive deep into medieval scholarship. I recommend looking at a variety of disciplines and topics. Here is where your friendly, neighborhood librarians can be of considerable help. Return to the public medievalists, and ask them questions.

Decide for Yourself

After engaging in this process, hopefully, you have formed your own ideas about the significance of studying the Middle Ages. It is good practice formally to articulate these ideas, perhaps in writing, to think through them so that they are clear and make sense to you before moving on to more and deeper medieval content.

Conclusion

The Connections among the Arts

[A]nyone with a mastery of only one field should provide for the student the means of accessing other fields; and should he have a mastery of multiple fields of knowledge, it is incumbent upon him to direct [the student] step by step [through the sciences] as he advances from one stage to another.

Al-Ghazâlî, "The Book of Knowledge," Iḥyāʾ ʿUlūm al-Dīn [The Revival of the Religious Sciences][1]

It is in the seven liberal arts, however, that the foundation of all learning is to be found [...] Therefore, those persons seem to me to be in error who, not appreciating the coherence among the arts, select certain of them for study, and leaving the rest untouched, think they can become perfect in these alone.

Hugh of Saint Victor, Didascalicon[2]

Hugh of Saint Victor is, of course, referencing the seven liberal arts represented by the trivium and the quadrivium, but his assertion is equally as valid to our modern understanding of the liberal arts. While we have examined the three categories or cultures of the modern liberal arts separately in this book, it is essential to remember that modes of knowledge rarely operate in isolation, rather, they serve to enhance and support each other—thus Al-Ghazâlî's admonition to teach-

---

1 Al-Ghazâlî, *Iḥyāʾ ʿUlūm al-Dīn*, trans. Honerkamp, 165.

2 Hugh of Saint Victor, *The Didascalicon*, trans. Taylor, 89.

ers to ensure students receive training in multiple disciplines. Appreciating, investigating, and applying the interconnectedness is the essence of being liberally educated—and the essence of studying the Middle Ages. Studying the literature of the period without studying history is only understanding part of the picture. Studying the science without studying religion is to ignore medieval worldviews.

Of the studies and ideas introduced in this book, the vast majority draw on methodologies and concepts from multiple fields. The way medieval studies disciplines build off of each other is reflective of how the liberal arts disciplines interact. Rather than being separate bodies of knowledge and sets of skills, the liberal arts cultures complement each other and work together to lead to important discoveries and, more importantly, to a more complete understanding of the human experience. Just as the various approaches to disability combine to form a whole, the liberal arts combine to provide insight into our whole existence. The researchers of the Dantean Anomaly commented that the "inclusion of humanities research clearly contributes to a better understanding of the social consequences of climate change in the past and to drawing conclusions for the future."[3] Climatologists are beginning to utilize a wide range of sources, including literature and storytelling, to map out a clearer understanding of historic climate. Stories are influenced by their environment, and the changes in weather and cataclysmic events like volcanic eruptions are of particular interest, especially when there are noticeable differences to everyday or seasonal life. It is through the blending of sources and methodologies that we learn the most about and from the past.

Another way to think about these interdisciplinary approaches is to reflect on the calls for modern medical professionals to embrace a more complete view of patients,

3 Leibniz Institute for Tropospheric Research, "Drought of the century in the Middle Ages—with parallels to climate change today?," *Phys.org*, January 5, 2021, https://phys.org/news/2021-01-drought-century-middle-ageswith-parallels.html.

evaluating them as humans, examining such factors that contribute to health as systemic racism, and recognizing the value of such therapies as art and music. We could learn from the medieval minds that did not compartmentalize the spiritual, social, and scientific, but rather considered and studied the whole human being. The Indigenous American medicine wheel, in use for thousands of years, provides a clear integration of the spiritual, mental, and physical to address issues of health and healing.

The life and writings of Robert Grosseteste serve as a final example of this integration. Bishop of Lincoln in the first half of the thirteenth century after serving as a lecturer and master at Oxford University (for which he helped systematize the curriculum), Grosseteste demonstrated an interest in all areas of study that affected human beings and wrote extensively on a number of subjects. He delved into theology and the bible, created sermons, and also studied philosophy, composing commentaries on Augustine, Aristotle, Avicenna, and Averroes. The influence of the latter also led him into medicine, science, and mathematics, writing works ranging from the scientific method and the nature of sounds and optics to comets, lines and angles, and celestial bodies. Further, he did not only compose commentaries and what we would call non-fiction. He also wrote the Anglo-Norman allegory *Le Château d'Amour* [Castle of Love] that blends theological and romance elements. In all of these cases, he united his understanding of the religious and philosophical with the physical and the scientific. Unsurprising, one of Grosseteste's works is *On the Liberal Arts* (*De artibus liberalibus*) in which he advocates for the moral necessity of a broad-based education, particularly for social reform.

What Robert Grosseteste and other medieval minds teach us is that our lives are far more interconnected than we sometimes believe. While we might spend more time studying one slice of knowledge than we do others, it is imperative to remember that the other pieces exist and inform our understanding. We can leave no study completely "untouched," and the study of the Middle Ages is an interdisciplinary wonderland.

CASE STUDIES IN MEDIEVAL LIBERAL ARTS
4. UNITING THE THREE
LIBERAL ARTS CULTURES

"Unclouding the Historical Rainbow"

An all-too-common response to modern fiction and literature that includes LGBTQIA+ people, especially any based on historical settings, is that "they shouldn't be included" because "they didn't exist back then." This view is quite patently incorrect. LGBTQIA+ individuals have existed throughout history. I will take a brief look at accounts from the ancient to medieval periods, countering the erroneous and harmful assertion that representation is in any way "inaccurate."

Let's address this idea of "historical accuracy" first. When you hear this phrase, be a little wary. Quite frequently, it gets used as an "academic-sounding" code to protest representation, whether that be in terms of gender or race or any other marginalized community. The argument, of course, rather quickly breaks down when you consider that no one seems to have a similar problem, for instance, with dragons in the medieval-esque *Game of Thrones* (and the fact that it is a work of *fiction*).

There are many misconceptions about gender roles in the past. It is popular to believe that there was "men's work" and "women's work" and never the twain shall meet. The truth is far more wonderfully complex in that labor, across time and geographies, was shared on a spectrum. A number of discoveries in the last few years alone question the long-held belief in the division of labor. For instance, pottery making—traditionally and automatically assumed to be "women's work." We have found, based upon the size of fingerprints, that thousand-year-old Puebloan pottery from the Southwest of the US appears to have been equally made by all genders.[4] And what about warriors? Those are all male, right? Espe-

---

4 Kanter, McKinney, Pierson, and Wester, "Reconstructing sexual divisions of labor."

cially Vikings! Due to this belief, when a Viking grave was discovered in Birka, Sweden, in 1878, with all the burial goods associated with a warrior, the skeleton was immediately dubbed male. Turns out, completely untrue. New technologies have identified the skeleton as female.[5] Book production in the Middle Ages—all male monks? Not according to the discovery of lapis lazuli in the teeth of an eleventh or twelfth-century German nun. Lapis lazuli was used in the illumination of manuscripts.[6]

These revelations—among many, many more—call into serious question the long-held belief of strict gender construction, not to mention the assumptions of researchers. What they don't tell us, on their own, is the lived experience of these individuals. With what gender did they identify? Were there other categories of gender recognized in society? In 2009, two 1600-year-old skeletons were found in Modena, Italy. The two were holding hands, prompting a romantic naming of "The Lovers of Modena" and, further, to be identified as a male and a female, despite the fact that the sex could not be determined. New work with dental peptides has revealed that the Lovers of Modena are both men.[7] While this discovery does not tell us the relationship of the two individuals, it does demonstrate the risk of assumptions, the danger of burying the identities of individuals and communities. Quite often, it is not the lack of evidence or sources from the distant past that affects how we perceive representation. Rather it is the conscious or unconscious bias of scholars, editors, researchers, publishers, and others, that prevent those sources from becoming common knowledge. Dr. Boyda Johnstone details how her work on medieval Arabic lesbianism, for instance, has been "beset with access problems and a distortion of original materials by prejudiced, conservative, and western-bi-

5 Price et al., "Viking warrior women?"

6 Radini et al., "Medieval women's early involvement."

7 Frederico Lugli et al., "Enamel peptides reveal the sex of the Late Antique 'Lovers of Modena'," *Scientific Reports* 9 (2019), https://doi.org//10.1038/s41598-019-49562-7.

ased editors."[8] Translators and editors have an inordinate amount of power to distort or suppress material with which they do not agree.

What we do know for a fact is that same-sex relationships certainly existed. One twelfth-century nun writes to another: "In you is all gentleness, all perfection, so my spirit languishes perpetually by your absence. You are devoid of the gall of any faithlessness, you are sweeter than milk and honey, you are peerless among thousands, I love you more than any."[9] As Dr. Erik Wade says, "These letters present a side of the Middle Ages that doesn't get taught as much: the Middle Ages wasn't an authoritarian, religiously dominated 'Dark Ages.' Medieval people produced educated, beautiful poetry, letters, and stories that portrayed a whole range of different attitudes towards gender and sexuality."[10]

Dr. Gabrielle Bychowski asks a question in the title of an article for *The Public Medievalist*: "Were there Transgender People in the Middle Ages?" In perhaps the best opening line of an article, she simply answers, "Yes." She does, of course, continue to answer this "absurd" question. If we base conclusions alone on the "biodiversity of the human species" with "0.6% of adults" identifying as trans, then "projected over the large numbers that make up the current populations of all those who live today—and all those who have ever lived—transgender and intersex people should be recognized as a significant and valuable part of human history."[11] As only one example, there are several saints' lives written in various parts of

---

8 Boyda Johnstone, "Vanishing Source Materials and Medieval Arabic Lesbianism, by Boyda Johnstone," *Whores of Yore, August* 23, 2019, https://www.thewhoresofyore.com/sex-history/vanishing-source-materials-and-medieval-arabic-lesbianism-by-boyda-johnstone.

9 Murray, "Twice Marginal and Twice Visible."

10 Anya Crittenton, "Love letter between nuns show the true story of queerness in the Middle Ages," *Gay Star News*, December 8, 2018, https://www.gaystarnews.com/article/queer-middle-ages/.

11 Bychowski, "Were There Transgender People in the Middle Ages?"

the medieval world, such as "The Life of Hilaria/Hilarion," that tell the stories of individuals assigned female at birth who then choose to live as males in monastic communities.[12] Dr. Roland Betancourt notes that "these figures were able to transform the secondary sex characteristics of the bodies through ascetic practice," that is the practice of deprivation of the body—such as limiting food intake—for religious purposes, which has such side effects as stopping menstruation, thereby contributing to physical transformation.[13]

Cross-dressing too was widely-known in the Middle Ages.[14] Perhaps the most popular figure is Joan of Arc, but she is far from the only example. The *Roman de Silence*, a thirteenth-century Old French romance, follows the title character who is born female, but due to some anxieties about inheritance, is announced to the public as a male. He lives as a male, learns how to be a knight, fighting in tournaments and earning renown in battle. Check out the modern retelling *The Story of Silence* by Alex Myers.[15]

One of my favorite stories about cross-dressing women is from the fourteenth-century English *Chronicle* by Henry Knighton. He describes "a troop of ladies...to the number of forty or sometimes fifty" would attend tournaments "dressed in parti-coloured tunics, of one colour on one side and a different one on the other, with short hoods, and liripipes wound about their heads like strings, with belts of gold and silver clasped about them, and even with the kind of knives called daggers slung low across their bellies, in pouches...paraded themselves at tournaments on fine chargers and other well-arrayed

---

12 See *Trans and Genderqueer Subjects in Medieval Hagiography, ed. Spencer-Hall* and Gutt.

13 Betancourt, "Transgender Lives in the Middle Ages."

14 See Hotchkiss, *Clothes Make the Man*.

15 Alex Myers, "What a 13th-Century Medieval Text Can Teach Us About Queerness and Gender," *Literary Hub*, June 22, 2021, https://lithub.com/what-a-13th-century-medieval-text-can-teach-us-about-queerness-and-gender/.

horses...and displayed their bodies."[16] Knighton takes pleasure in announcing that they were punished by God visiting "cloudbursts, and thunder and flashing lightning, and tempests of astonishing violence upon them." He does not make an explicit connection, but, in the next paragraph, he turns to "a general plague [the Bubonic] upon mankind throughout the world," perhaps insinuating these cross-dressing ladies were at least partially responsible. Dr. Sonia Drimmer finds it interesting that Knighton wrote this episode down at all, speculating that "the chronicler seems to have expected his audience would see women wanting to perform as men (and assert their sexual agency by 'displaying their bodies') as entirely plausible, particularly in a privileged space that was designed to assert rigid gender roles."[17] She even posits that the specular nature of these activities aligns them closely with drag performances.

Recognizing the presence of gender fluidity and diversity in the past is integral to debunking pernicious arguments supporting the erasure of individuals and their heritages. We need to lift the clouds from the historical rainbow.

---

16 Henry Knighton, *Knighton's Chronicle: 1337–1396*, trans. G. H. Martin (Oxford: Oxford University Press, 1996), 94–95.

17 Matthew Gabriele, "The Medieval Women in Drag Who Maybe Caused the Black Death (But Really Didn't)," *Forbes*, February 10, 2019, https://www.forbes.com/sites/matthewgabriele/2019/02/10/medieval-women-in-drag/?sh=479428b147a3.

Further Reading

Al-Ghazâlî. "The Book of Knowledge": Book 1 of the *Iḥyā'Ulūm al-Dīn: The Revival of the Religious Sciences*. Translated by Kenneth Honerkamp. Louisville: Fons Vitae, 2015.

"Ancestral Technologies and Climate Change." *The Mountain Institute*. Accessed April 15, 2022. http://mountain.org/ancestral-technologies-climate-change/.

Arano, Luisa Cogliati. *The Medieval Health Handbook: Tacuinum Sanitatis*. Translated by Oscar Ratti and Adele Westbrook. New York: Braziller, 1976.

Betancourt, Roland. "Transgender Lives in the Middle Ages through Art, Literature, and Medicine." The Getty Iris. https://www.getty.edu/art/exhibitions/outcasts/downloads/betancourt_transgender_lives.pdf.

Bychowski, Gabrielle. "Were There Transgender People in the Middle Ages?" *The Public Medievalist*. November 1, 2018. https://www.publicmedievalist.com/transgender-middle-ages/.

Caravans of Gold, Fragments in Time: Art, Culture and Exchange Across Medieval Saharan Africa, edited by Kathleen Bickford Berzock. Evanston: Block Museum of Art, 2019.

Conrad, David. *Empires of Medieval West Africa: Ghana, Mali, and Songhay*. New York: Facts on File, 2005.

Disability in the Middle Ages, edited by Joshua R. Eyler. Burlington: Ashgate, 2010.

Duricy, Michael. "Black Madonnas: Origin, History, Controversy." *All About Mary*. University of Dayon. Accessed April 15, 2022. https://udayton.edu/imri/mary/b/black-madonnas-origin-history-controversy.php.

Falk, Seb. *The Light Ages: The Surprising Story of Medieval Science*. New York: Norton, 2020.

Fauvelle, François-Xavier. *The Golden Rhinoceros: Histories of the African Middle Ages*. Princeton: Princeton University Press, 2018.

Frankopan, Peter. "Why We Need to Think About the Global Middle Ages." *Journal of Medieval Worlds* 1, no. 1 (2019): 5–10.

Gabriele, Matthew, and David M. Perry. *The Bright Ages: A New History of Medieval Europe*. New York: Harper, 2021.

Graham, Elyse. "What I Learned on Medieval Twitter." *Public Books*. July 24, 2019. https://www.publicbooks.org/what-i-learned-on-medieval-twitter/.

Green, Monica H. "Plagues Past, Paths Forward." *Arc Humanities Press Blog*. July 29, 2019. https://www.arc-humanities.org/blog/2019/07/23/plagues-past-paths-forward/.

Greenfield, Mark Steven. *Black Madonna*. William Turner Gallery. issuu, 2020. https://issuu.com/turnergallery/docs/mark_steven_greenfield.

Hamilton, Bernard. *The Leper King and His Heirs: Baldwin IV and the Crusader Kingdom of Jerusalem*. Cambridge: Cambridge University Press, 2000.

Harvey, John. *Mediaeval Gardens*. London: Batsford, 1981.

Heng, Geraldine. *The Invention of Race in the European Middle Ages*. Cambridge: Cambridge University Press, 2018.

Hotchkiss, Valerie R. *Clothes Make the Man: Female Cross Dressing in Medieval Europe*. New York: Routledge, 1999.

Hsy, Jonathan, and Julie Orlemanski. "Race and Medieval Studies: A Partial Bibliography." *Postmedieval* 8 (2017): 500–31. https://doi.org/10.1057/s41280-017-0072-0.

Hugh of Saint Victor. *The Didascalicon of Hugh of Saint Victor: A Medieval Guide to the Arts*. Translated by Jerome Taylor. New York: Columbia University Press, 1991.

Ibn Battuta in Black Africa. Translated and edited by Said Hamdun and Noel King. Princeton: Wiener, 2003.

Ibn Khaldun. *The Muqaddimah*. Translated by Franz Rosenthal. http://www.muslimphilosophy.com/ik/Muqaddimah/.

Jain, Ravi, and Kevin Clark. *The Liberal Arts Tradition*. Camp Hill: Classical Academic Press, 1984.

John of Salisbury. *The Metalogicon*. Translated by Daniel D. McGarry. Mansfield Centre: Martino, 2015.

Kagen, Jerome. *The Three Cultures: Natural Sciences, Social Sciences, and the Humanities in the 21st Century*. Cambridge: Cambridge University Press, 2009.

Klimek, Kimberly, et al. *Global Medieval Contexts 500-1500: Connections and Comparisons*. New York: Routledge, 2021.

Kurlansky, Mark. *Salt: A World History*. New York: Penguin, 2003.

Lieberman, Benjamin and Elizabeth Gordon. *Climate Change in Human History: Prehistory to the Present*. New York: Bloomsbury, 2018.

Liu, Xinru. *The Silk Road in World History*. Oxford: Oxford University Press, 2010.

Maimonides. *On Poisons and the Protection Against Lethal Drugs*. Translated by Gerrit Bos. Provo: Brigham Young University, 2009.

McC. Gatch, Milton. "The Medievalist and Cultural Literacy." *Speculum* 66, no. 3 (1991): 591–604.

Medieval Academy of America. "The Mother of All Pandemics: The State of Black Death Research in the Era of COVID-19." *Medieval Academy.* May 17, 2020. https://youtu.be/VzqR1S8cbX8.

Middle English Legends of Women Saints. Edited by Sherry L. Reames. Kalamazoo: Medieval Institute Publications, 2003.

Murray, Jacqueline. "Twice Marginal and Twice Visible: Lesbians in the Middle Ages." *Handbook of Medieval Sexuality*, edited by Vern L. Bullough and James Brundage, 191–223. New York: Routledge, 2000.

Nasr, Seyyed Hossein. *Science and Civilization in Islam.* Cambridge, MA: Harvard University Press, 1968. Reprint, Chicago: ABC, 2001.

Pandemic Disease in the Medieval World: Rethinking the Black Death, edited by Monica H. Green, The Medieval Globe 1. Kalamazoo: Arc Humanities Press, 2015.

Reilly, Maura. *Curatorial Activism: Towards an Ethics of Curating.* London: Thames & Hudson, 2018.

Saslow, Eli. *Rising Out of Hatred.* New York: Doubleday, 2018.

Small, Helen. *The Value of the Humanities.* Oxford: Oxford University Press, 2016.

Snyder, Sharon L. and David T. Mitchell. *Cultural Locations of Disability.* Chicago: University of Chicago Press, 2006.

Sturtevant, Paul B. "Race, Racism, and the Middle Ages: Tearing Down the 'Whites Only' Medieval World." *The Public Medievalist.* February 7, 2017. https://www.publicmedievalist.com/race-racism-middle-ages-tearing-whites-medieval-world.

Toswell, M. J. *Today's Medieval University.* Kalamazoo: Arc Humanities Press, 2017.

Trans and Genderqueer Subjects in Medieval Hagiography, edited by Alicia Spencer-Hall and Blake Gutt. Amsterdam: Amsterdam University Press, 2021.

Turner, Howard R. *Science in Medieval Islam*. Austin: University of Texas Press, 1995.

Tyerman, Christopher. *The World of the Crusades*. New Haven: Yale University Press, 2019.

Utz, Richard. *Medievalism: A Manifesto*. Kalamazoo: Arc Humanities Press, 2017.

Van Engen, John. "Introduction." In *Learning Institutionalized: Teaching in the Medieval University*, edited by John Van Engen, 1–4. Notre Dame: University of Notre Dame Press, 2000.

Virgin Lives and Holy Deaths, edited by Jocelyn Wogan-Browne and Glyn S. Burgess. London: Everyman, 1996.

"What Is Liberal Education?" *Association of American Colleges & Universities*. Accessed April 15, 2022. https://www.aacu.org/leap/what-is-a-liberal-education.

Whitaker, Cord J., ed. "Making Race Matter in the Middle Ages." Special issue, *Postmedieval* 6, no. 1 (2015).

Why the Humanities Matter Today: In Defense of Liberal Education, edited by Lee Trepanier and Kirk Fitzpatrick. Lanham: Lexington, 2017.

Zakaria, Fareed. *In Defense of a Liberal Education*. New York: Norton, 2015.

Printed and bound by CPI Group (UK) Ltd, Croydon, CR0 4YY

13/04/2025

14656453-0002